Living
On This Water Planet
Called Earth

Living
On this Water Planet
Called Earth

Dexter MacBride

INLANDIA

Living on this Water Planet Called Earth is an original publication of Inlandia Press. This work has never before appeared in book form.

INLANDIA press
b. a.   o k l a h o m a

First Trade Printing: August 2010

Manufactured in the United States of America.

Table of Contents

1

The Magic of Water: Mythology & Facts

*I do set my bow in the cloud, and it shall be for a token of a covenant
between me and the earth and every living creature.*
-- *Ancient Hebrew scripture*

Whether ancient Hebrew scripture or modern rainbow, the symbolism is rich: flood waters prevailed, the fountains of the deep and the windows of heaven were stopped; the rainbow became a token of agreement between an Almighty, Mankind and all Creatures.

As we see rainbows today, we understand, thanks to Isaac Newton, light is refracted and separated into various wavelengths; rainbows are created by the natural prism of water particles.

How surprising it is that water, so dominant on our planet, (70.8% water; 29.2% land) did not become our "ID" as *The Water Planet!* It's hard to believe that our potable water is so relatively scarce. Of all earth's water, 97.3% lies in the seas/oceans (saltwater); 2.1% is in ice caps and glaciers; 0.59% in groundwater; 0.01% in rivers and lakes. More than a billion persons – some 20% of those on our globe – do not have access to an adequate supply of potable water.

The ancient Greeks have given our culture a rich mythology. They conjectured they inhabited a flat, circular disc-like world crossed by an east-west River (the Mediterranean) and encircled by a vast ocean that was uncharted, unknown, and inhabited by monsters of the deep. Entrance to the western "unknown" was at present-day Gibraltar where the mammoth monolith in the Strait marked the Pillars of Hercules.

Hercules is the central figure of one of the earth's great myths. He was forced to meet twelve challenges called the Labors of Hercules. Of the twelve (he met and overcame all), one of the most curious was the Cleansing of the Augean Stables. King Augeas had three thousand oxen and their stalls had not been cleansed for thirty years. The aqueous solution: Hercules diverted the rivers Alpheus and Peneus into the stalls, cleansing them completely in one day.

The magic properties of water and the facts surrounding the administration, delivery, use and protection of potable water sources is a worldwide concern at all levels of government; national, regional, state, city, and community.

The U.S. is the third largest consumer of water in the world (India and China the most). About half of U.S. citizens live within 50 miles of an ocean. Off California's coast, some 20,000 square miles of Pacific coastal waters are closed to fishing as a protective preservation measure. California's principal "salt water wonder" is Monterey Canyon, close to the shoreline, and about twice the depth of the Grand Canyon. Of note is the fact that 84 million acres have been dedicated (Y2000) as a nature preserve called the Hawaii Islands Coral Reef Ecosystem Reserve.

Of concern in the United States is environmental damage done to scarce resources of fresh water in the country's rivers and lakes. The state of California is reported to be putting more cancer-causing pollutants into rivers, bays and ocean waters than any other state (Y2000).

The National Resources Defense Council reports sewer spills and polluted runoff forced closing of California's beaches 4500 times in 2002. Orange County, California led the nation in such closings.

Pollution of monumental proportions impacts the entire midsection of the United States. For example, the mighty Mississippi River, some 1000 miles in length and third longest on the planet, pours into the Gulf of Mexico dumping millions of tons of fertilizer runoff from farmlands and waste releases from industrial plants and creating a vast dead zone of some 7000 square miles where nothing can live.

The Mississippi transformed de facto into the nation's largest sewer system!

Egypt's Nile River presents a similar picture, dumping fertilizer and industrial waste into the Mediterranean. The Rio Grande – the storied U.S. - Mexico waterway – is exhausted by use and drought and dumps vestigial waste into the Gulf of Mexico.

Southern California offers an instructive window into the water problem impacting a densely populated area in a semi-desert. Seventeen million people, residing in 6 counties, are served by a giant water district with interrelated ties involving county, city, state, and federal agencies responsible for prompt potable water delivery. So powerful are social requirements for housing, jobs, health, fire and police protection, recreation, and transportation facilities, that often a potable water supply is assumed to be a given.

Legal battles over water rights never cease, particularly in regard to the Colorado River. Solutions have prompted unique proposals, including "fallowing" of some 30,000 acres of high-production irrigated farmland; saving California's inland Salton Sea, as a major sanctuary for migratory fowl using the great Pacific Flyway; a vast water storage program in the Cadiz Aquatic Storage supply and East Mesa Aquifer; and U.S.-Mexico-Colorado delta region efforts to prevent desiccation of parched wetlands, riparian forest, and wildlife areas.

A 2003 proposal to merge Northern California's water sources (the State Water Project and Federal Central Valley

Project) with the Southern Metropolitan Water District and other major districts has been achieved, assuring an ample, secured water supply and statewide distribution, and achieved by provision of sufficient reservoir storage capacity and adequate pumping systems.

Despite the agreement and assurance that California's water battles are over for years to come, recognition of the litigious climate and the perception that water is California's gold reminds doubters of the fabled punishment of Sisyphus, who was committed forever to roll a great stone up a hill only to see it slip and roll down again, and again, and again.

One has but to look at other countries to understand the strain being placed upon major water sources.

In Mexico, Lake Chapala stretches some 50 miles across the states of Jalisco and Michoacán. Described as the "jewel oasis" in the country's parched west central highlands, Lake Chapala now contains less than 20% of its capacity. The major reason is due to the lake's serving as the principal source of potable drinking water for Guadalajara, a large city 30 miles to the north. The aqueous jewel now resembles a puddle. The former 35-foot water level is now around 4.5 feet. Historian Armando Hermosillo wrote: "The Lake is a god. It is the father and mother that inspire us. If the Lake dies, everything will die. This place will be a Hell." Residents of the lakeside village of Ajijic echo the sentiment and concern.

It is interesting to contrast the relatively small Lake Chapala with remote Siberian Lake Baikal, located in the Republic of Buryatia in the Russian Federation. Lake Baikal lies northerly of the Mongolian Republic and is some 400 miles in length and about 5,700 feet in depth. It is estimated to hold about one-fifth of the Earth's fresh water. Irkutsk, a modern city with a half-million people, is located at the southerly end of the Lake. Trans Siberian Railway representatives consider Lake Baikal a favorite stop.

In China, a massive multi-billion dollar water diversion project is underway: to pump water from the green south to the arid north. Three great north-south aqueducts will carry Yangtze River water to Beijing and other major northern cities by 2010. About one-half of China's population will be served by the system. It is estimated 48 billion tons of water annually will reach the north via the three north-south channels.

At the Malay Peninsula, the island nation of Singapore and its population of 2 million are facing a potable water availability problem with the Federation of Malaysia in a most unique fashion. Singapore's Public Utilities Board introduced an assured potable water supply to its population through a product branded NEWater, which is drinking water created from treated waste water.

Increasing populations place even greater pressure upon existing potable water resources. Desalination is a significant alternative source on the horizon and may be the only such source. Desalination plants, sometimes called – desal plants – will be built in California and other thirsty states and may enhance and clarify the relationship of humankind and sodium chloride.

Worldwide, there are some 13.000 desal plants currently producing eight billion gallons of potable water per day. In Tampa, Florida a $198 million dollar plant is currently operational with a target production of 25 million gallons daily. The entire U.S. desalinates some 230 million cubic meter per year, which is less than 1% of the water in use.

Desalination may provide the most significant long range proposal to produce a new source of potable water for California, one of the most populous states in the US and as a governmental structure represents perhaps the 5th largest economy in the world. It may well prove to be a fiscally viable complement to river, lake and groundwater sources. Desalination is receiving attention in the cities of Carlsbad, Oceanside, Long Beach, Playa del Rey and Dana Point. Some water districts are offering substantial incentives for research and planning. Reverse Osmosis (RO) appears to be a major key to financially successful production.

The California Coastal Commission, a state agency, is studying desalination potential and impacts. It approved a Long Beach project which began operations in 2005 at the Hayes Generating Station producing 300,000 gallons per day and studying energy consumption, funded by $8 million in state and federal grants and $7 million raised by Long Beach Water Department rate payers.

Concerns by environmentalists over the implementation of desalination include possible destruction of marine life, turning public resources into private business enterprises, burdens on local infrastructure, harm to sensitive habitats, and possible harm to fish, plankton, and larvae.

It is a concomitant and strange fact that oceanic underwater research is at a virtual standstill.

In 1962, Jacques Cousteau assembled a skilled underwater team whose members lived 40 feet underwater off the coast of Marseille, France in a lab called Conshelf. The U.S. Navy launched Sealab in 1964, and a doomed third launch took humans 600 feet deep before the death of a diver caused the program to be abandoned. During the 1960's and 70's, some 65 programs involving life in undersea labs were conducted with some producing remarkable success.

A sea lab called Aquarius began construction in 1985 and currently rests on a coral reef about 4 miles offshore in the Florida Keys. Aquarius weighs 91 tons and is managed jointly by the National Oceans and Atmospheric Administration and the University of North Carolina-Wilmington. The project has an approximate $1 million dollar annual budget.

It is well worth pondering explorer Cousteau's explanation of his fascination with the underwater worlds of the oceans.

"The gist of my life's work," he wrote, "has been to free man from the bondage of the surface, permit him to live in the ocean." Cousteau imagined men of a new breed that were beginning to evolve, a species who would become men-of-the-water, creatures of inner space.

Why no further apparent achievement beneath the oceans? Perhaps it is due to the success of NASA and its outer space ventures - or could it be that an idea has been spread that the oceans and seas are being trashed? Who wants to venture out to explore mankind's vast garbage dump, a world stripped of plentiful fish and other sea life?

The concept of the oceans as a vast aqueous disposal area may seem overstated. However, consider a representative problem in the luxury cruise ships that travel the oceans and seas.

These "floating cities" can dump raw sewage beyond the three mile limit. Carrying perhaps 4000-5000 passengers, one ship may generate 210,000 gallons of sewage in a week in addition to a million gallons of so-called "gray water" from sinks, dishwashers, and showers, as well as upwards of 37,000 gallons of bilge water and 8 tons of solid wastes.

Wordsworth, in his sonnet "The World is too much with us," asked for glimpses of life that would make him less forlorn. He wished to "have sight of Proteus rising from the sea, or hear Old Triton blow his wreathed horn."

Byron, in "Apostrophe to the Ocean," had this version:

"Roll on, thou deep and dark blue Ocean, roll! Ten thousand fleets sweep over three in vain; Man marks the earth with ruin, his control Stops with the shore."

Any contemplative perspective or review of water in the contiguous states of presents a dazzling array, much like looking into a kaleidoscope of childhood memory, the bits of colored glass in the small rotating tube of the wonderful toy corroborating the origin of its name: from the Greek terms, *kalos* = beautiful and *eidos* = form.

Behold! 250,000 rivers; 2,200 square miles of lakes; some 5,000 square miles of estuaries! And More! The rivers have some 70,000 dams!

A special cautionary note: In California's 1928 St. Francis Dam disaster, the dam located about 40 miles north of the city of Los Angeles collapsed, killing more than 400 persons in one of the worst disasters in state history. The California Dam Safety Program is between a rock and a hard place according to its officials, because the inspection of the estimated 1,200 public and private dams over 25 feet high – excepting federal dams – must be halted. State budget shortfalls caused funding for the inspections to be ended.

The High Plains Aquifer is one of the greatest natural resources in the contiguous U.S. and covers about 175,000 square miles. The underground water serves about 2,000,000 people and 13 million acres of crop land. Some 7 trillion gallons of water are withdrawn annually. Reports warn that by the year 2025, major portions of the aquifer may be totally depleted.

In many cultures, the relationship of Man to certain rivers has to be characterized by awe, pride, admiration and fear. Even a cursory review will illustrate the emotional power and wonder involved. Despite an unceasing encroachment, an overwhelming sense of partnership and enchantment has moved Man to extol, glorify, and worship the shining waters of life.

In mythology, the Greeks presented the somber vision of the River Styx, the river over which the dead were carried into the lower world. Charon the Ferryman was responsible for the solemn transport.

From the Romans of 49 BC we inherited a verbal yardstick which measures decision-making: "Crossing the Rubicon." The Rubicon is a relatively minor river in northern Italy. Julius Caesar decided to cross it with military forces and a civil war ensued. Caesar's decision was considered a monumentally decisive act – so much so that the phrase remains with us today. Make a decision; cross the Rubicon.

The relatively modern "discovery" of the Sargasso Sea, initially reported by Columbus in his description of the West Indies voyage, contributes to man's fascination with ocean waters. Theories arose about the possibility that people from Carthage reached this mysterious "sea" located in the North Atlantic between the Azores and the West Indies. Those of us entranced by the story of old deserted ships drawn into the Sargasso and endlessly, slowly, and silently moving in giant ghostlike circular patterns must now face reality. The supposed maritime graveyard enshrouded in constant mist has been totally discredited. The Sargasso Sea exists however, as an area with an abundance of seaweed floating on its comparatively calm waters.

An unending aggression-response mode between Water and Man exists on this planet.

In the Netherlands, the total land area approximates 14,000 square miles. About two-fifths of Holland is below sea level; land loss by erosion and flooding is omnipresent. Dykes and sand dunes prevent tidal inundation three major rivers flow through the water-dominated nation. Heavy rains can cause a reverse problem in the low-lying polders, which are areas reclaimed from the sea and protected by dykes. How is excess water returned to the sea? Windmills. We have inherited pictures of windmills from classic literature, especially Cervantes' Don Quixote. Too, we recall the story of the small Dutch child, with his finger plunged into a dyke to prevent a disastrous flood.

Another chapter in man's confrontation with the waters of the oceans is written in Venice, Italy, an enchanting city of lagoons, canals and beautiful structures. For decades a force in worldwide water trade, it is now facing ominous encroachment by the sea it has loved and cherished. Whether the Jewel of the Mediterranean is sinking or the surrounding sea is rising, the threat is omnipresent. One cannot resist comparison with Mexico City, a magnificent capitol city. Originally called Tenochtitlan, the city of the Aztecs was founded on a lake. At the principal square, *la Plaza de la Constitucion*, portions of the magnificent cathedral are visibly sinking because of steady depletion of underlying water base drained for public use.

England's famous Thames River presents an additional perspective in the consideration of the beneficent symbiosis which can characterize man-water relationships. The Thames is a modest river, perhaps 210 miles in length. It is a major source of London's potable water supply. Curiously, the

Thames is called the Isis River in the Oxford area. A tidal river, its flooding periods around London coincide with high tides. The Thames watershed comprises some 3,800 square miles and is protected from pollution by the Thames Conservancy and a series of locks controls the river flow. The British and the Thames are an orderly partnership.

When considering man's awe of rivers, the tendency to glorify - even worship - the shining water is understandable. India's River Ganges evokes such reverence. The river receives drainage from the central Himalayas during the course of its 1,500 mile long expanse. The religious significance of the Ganges cannot be overstated. It is probably greater than that of any river on earth. The many places of pilgrimage along the river testify to the religious fervor and force it evokes. It is the Holy River, sacred to some 350,000,000 Hindus. The extreme "holiness" of the Ganges arises from the belief that the Ganges derives its waters from Shiva, the Hindu god of destruction and reproduction; Brahma, the Creator; and Vishnu, the Preserver.

In terms of majestic might, it is the Amazon River in South America which almost overwhelms understanding. It is the world's largest river by volume, drainage, and basin area. It was named by the Spanish explorer, Orellena, for a battle involving Indian tribes in which he claimed to observe tribal women fighting side-by-side with men like *Amazons*.

The drainage area includes 2,722,000 square miles encompassing forty percent of South America. The Amazon flows some 3,915 miles from the Andes to the Atlantic Ocean, and is surpassed in length only by the Nile at 4,132 miles. The Amazon River's discharge is seven times greater than that of the Mississippi. Its mighty flow encompasses nearly one-fifth of all the fresh water that runs off the earth's surface. Seventeen of its major tributaries have lengths exceeding 1000 miles.

Consider the aqueous wonderland of Florida's Everglades, an area diminished by half its original size, yet still embracing about 2.4 million acres of saw grass, islands, and sloughs. It represents a man-contrived Gordian knot of political, fiscal, environmental, and social struggles being contested primarily by sugar barons, environmentalists and government agencies.

At the heart of contention is the Everglades Forever Act of 1995, supported by many from whom preservation of the Everglades is a sacred trust. On the other side are companies and groups managing a sugar cane cultivation that represents one of Florida's largest cash crops. It is an industry generating an estimated $500 million dollars annually, producing about 28% of US sugar production.

The *casus belli*: half of the Everglades has been lost, initially through encroaching houses, roads, golf courses and related intrusions, and secondly, by continuing runoff containing high amounts of phosphorus flowing from the sugar cane fields as a pollutant.

Since the 1940's, flood control, navigation, pipelines, irrigation, drainage, and the burgeoning population's need for potable water have caused a re-plumbing of the Everglades. It involves 1000 miles of canals, 700 miles of levees, and 16 huge pumping stations. It is not surprising 68 animal species are endangered or threatened by the pollutants and alteration of the natural watercourse.

Legislators in Florida recognize that the Everglades area as a habitat and water resource is in peril. Little wonder that an $8 billion dollar project proposal for restoring the Everglades is on Tallahassee agendas!

In Louisiana, environmental issues represent a monumental challenge. Since 1932, the state has lost 1,000 square miles of land to unceasing erosion of the Mississippi River basin. Some 400 remedial mud terraces have been created in the last 17 years to combat erosion at a cost of $400 million dollars. An almost unbelievable proposal advocated as a solution to the basin problem is a plan to unleash the Mississippi River. The proposed 30 year project is estimated to have a price tag of $14 billion dollars. The preservation of the delta region is of enormous importance to the entire state. Louisiana officials estimate the wetlands coast loses a land area the size of a football field every 38 minutes. The storied City of New Orleans, thought to be protected by an intricate system of pumps, pipes and levees, is still recovering from the inundation caused by Hurricane Katrina in 2005.

The nation's largest river basin swamp located in south central Louisiana, west of Baron Rouge, was first settled by the Acadians, French-Canadian Catholic refugees expelled by the British in 1755 who settled the high grounds and bayous.

Flooding in 1927 killed hundreds and destroyed some 40,000 buildings through 16 million acres in Arkansas, Kentucky, Louisiana, Mississippi, and Tennessee. Following the devastation, the U.S. Corps of Engineers invested $2 billion dollars in flood control measures. Canals and some 450 miles of levees were created, and more than 100 million cubic yards of earth were dredged as part of the control structure at the juncture of the Mississippi and the Atchafalaya rivers.

In 1984, Congress authorized the U.S. Corp of Engineers to undertake a new approach: unplug bayous, cut sediment gaps along high banks and canals, and preserve thousands of acres with environmental easements – measures taken to protect treasured ecosystems in the Atchafalaya Project and preserve the historical Cajun community lifestyle.

Following decades-long efforts to organize, manage, and improve the natural environment, the dramatic and drastic changes of direction in the States of Florida and Louisiana herald the reality and realization that man's efforts – although intended as beneficial – may be, can be, and in some cases have been counter-productive.

This reality represents a massive paradigm shift. A new relationship between Man and Water in the states of Florida and Louisiana is being honored in the process.

2

The Fertile Crescent

For 8000 years Iraq and its neighbors led the world as the source of most things embodied in the term 'civilization.' Technology, ideas, and power flowed outward from Iraq to Europe and eventually to America. Iraq's decline holds lessons the world should heed.
-- *UCLA Prof. Jared Diamond*

The nation of Iraq, brutalized, demoralized and now diminished by years of despotic rule, is now emerging from a pre-emptive military strike-invasion conducted by the United States of America.

The tyrannical Baath leadership has been removed. Iraq's infrastructure is in significant disarray. The U.S. – with assistance from several nations and international organizations – is now working to restore public services, repair damaged structures, strengthen rehabilitation resolve, re-introduce public participation in constructive civil governance.

As the historical heart of major cultures and civilizations, the Mesopotamia and the Babylon of ancient times, the so-called Fertile Crescent of the Tigris-Euphrates, why is Iraq no longer the mighty, magnificent, and wealthy nation is was?

Why the decline from acknowledged Zenith to a derided Nadir?

Is it the inexorable function of time or the imperative of history that cultures and civilizations emerge, grow, flourish, disintegrate, and die?

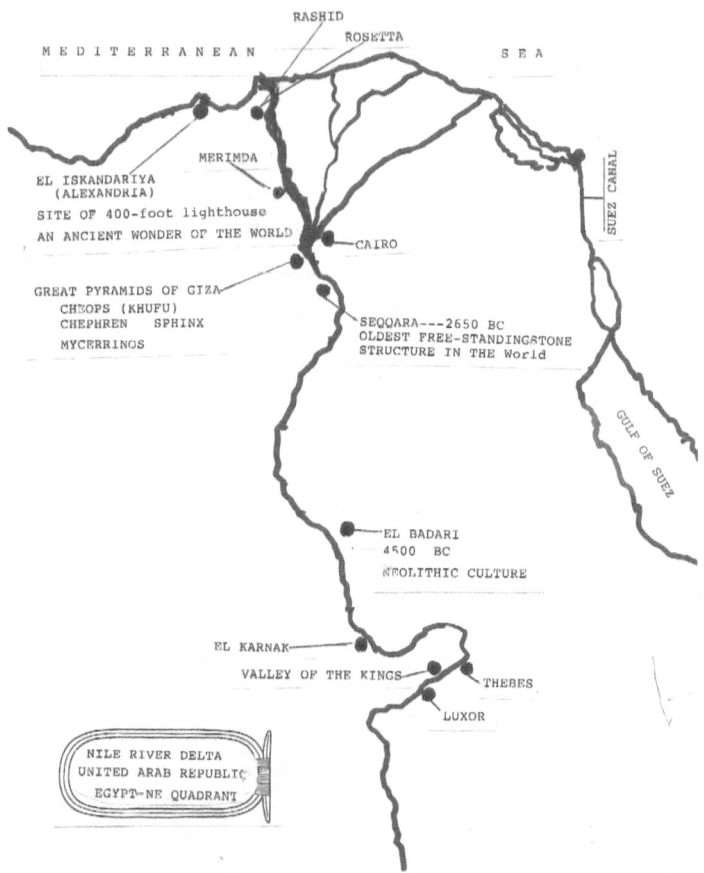

"The average age of the world's great civilizations has been two hundred years," wrote Alexander Tyler, an eighteenth century scholar, who traced the course "from bondage to spiritual faith; from spiritual faith to great courage; from courage to liberty; from liberty to abundance; from abundance to complacency; from complacency to apathy; from apathy to dependence; from dependence back to bondage."

Tyler's stages of change and 200 year civilization life span embracing a Nadir-Zenith-Nadir process with near religious certitude have been supplanted by historical and sociological explorations based on wider perspectives.

Culture is now understood to imply ways of living created by humans and transmitted from generation to generation. Civilization indicates the type of culture and society of specific group, and an advanced state of human society.

Implicit in the terms is a vexing generality. Lewis Carroll's *Through the Looking Glass* introduced the "portmanteau word," or a word with two meanings.

Iraq, whether examined from the perspective of culture or civilization, presents the same Zenith-to-Nadir picture. Jared Diamond noted how difficult it is to reconcile and understand Iraq's "Fertile Crescent" of world leadership, contrasted with its current infertile condition. Environmental degradation, deforestation, overgrazing, irrigation destruction, and salination, along with military impacts from Macedonians and Mongols to World Wars I and II, are conducive to poverty, health crises, civil unrest, illiteracy, factional disputes (Shiites, Sunnis, Kurds, Turkmen, Yazidis), and despotic rule.

Disastrous environmental impacts bombarding Iraq in the twentieth century included wetlands desiccation by drainage of 90% of the vast southern marshlands and lakes between the Tigris and Euphrates rivers, an area twice the size of Florida. It is interesting to note that some scholars consider the area to be the historic location of the Biblical Garden of Eden.

For some 5000 years this wetlands area teemed with fish and birds and humans; thousands of Shiite Muslims traveled the waterways. By Baath government fiat, wetlands drainage was subverted in order to deprive political opponents of their livelihood and traditional lifestyles.

Nourished by the Tigris and Euphrates rivers, the Fertile Crescent provided the Middle East with a treasured agricultural product: dates. The arrival of each year's date harvest was eagerly anticipated. Government imposed destruction of some six million date palms from a total of nine million in Basra alone brought trouble for Shiite Muslims who were targeted and crushed under the Hussein-Baath fist. Ultimately, some thirty million date palms were destroyed in 30 years.

It is helpful – and in the case of Iraq – necessary to ask: Why did Iraq decline? Why has it fallen from high cultural status? What vast unseen forces were at play? Greek mythology presents the following scenario of Omnipotence: Clotho, Lachesis and Atropos (daughters of Themis, who represented the personification of Justice) were responsible for the destiny of all persons in ancient Greece. Clotho was spinner of the Thread of Life; Lachesis measured the length of the Thread; Atropos was responsible for cutting the Thread.

In the first half of the 21st century, three pioneering scholars preferred new concepts and perspectives concerning the Life Threads of cultures and civilizations. Their monumental works created storms of praise, criticism, and rebuttal. Published studies are invaluable in assisting efforts to understand the histories of Iraq, Mesopotamia (translated literally as "Middle of the Rivers"), the Fertile Crescent, and the Arab World.

The larger question concerns the structural concept explaining and clarifying the origin, rise, success, decline, and disintegration of the world's cultures and civilizations.

Summations describing three world-view analyses include *The Decline of the West*, by Oswald Spengler (1926). Described as a volcanically assertive philosophy of history, Spengler emphasizes a major basic idea in the parallelism of organically living cultures while discarding concepts of history expressed in the usage of categories such as ancient, medieval, and modern, which dominate our current world view of history.

Essentially, Spengler views the Western-European idea of history as a Ptolemaic system, one that considers the Earth as the center of the universe. His eloquent advocacy of a Copernican viewpoint permits equal recognition of the cultures of India, Babylon, China, Egypt, Arabia, and Mexico. In consequence, it is suggested that every culture has its own civilization, that every civilization is the "inevitable destiny of the culture." It is proposed that our Western culture achieved civilization status in the 19th century.

Three concepts under-grid Spengler's notion of civilization: emergence of a World City (megalopolis), creation of Province (subsidiary to the World City); and the creation of Money, described by Spengler as "an inorganic and abstract magnitude, entirely disconnected from the fruitful earth and primitive values."

His morphology of history includes:

1   Contemporary Spiritual Epochs: a time sequence of Spring, Summer, Autumn, and Winter
2   Contemporary Cultural Epochs: details of pre-cultural periods from which the civilization emerges
3   Contemporary Political Epochs: examining early and late periods of the development of cultures and civilizations.

Spengler's coruscating visions in *Decline of the West* include the idea that man lacks the freedom to reach "to this or to that, but the freedom to do the necessary or to do nothing. And a task that historic necessity has set *will* be accomplished with the individual or against him." He concludes with the Latin phrase, *Ducunt Fata volentem, nolentem trahunt*, or "Fate leads the willing, drags the unwilling."

Another analysis of culture and civilization is that of Pitirim A. Sorokin, in his work *The Crisis of Our Age* (1941).

Based on his 4-volume work *Social and Cultural Dynamics*, Sorokin describes the twilight of sensate culture and society, contending that individual culture is not mortal, that cultures are not predestined to mature, decline, and die. He postulates three great eras in major cultures and civilizations: Ideational,

Idealistic, and Sensate. (We in the Western Culture are experiencing an exhaustion of our sensate era).

Effectiveness of each era can be examined and evaluated by such components as fine arts, truth, ethics and law, organization, economics, criminality, mental disease, and tragic dualism.

In a concluding commentary, Sorokin contemplates the final sensate days of some six hundred years: "We are seemingly between two epochs: the dying Sensate culture of our magnificent yesterday and the coming Ideational Culture of the creative tomorrow."

Similarly, Sorokin concludes *Crisis of Our Age* with a Latin phrase: *Benedictus qui venit in Nominee Domini*, or "Blessed is he who comes in the name of the Lord."

A personal parenthetical: I was a very young man when I first met Professor Sorokin, then Chairman of the Department of Sociology at Harvard University. The floor of his study was crowded with piles of books, and the work desk was equally crowded. He moved from pile to pile, taking notes. Suddenly he stopped, turned, and asked if I understood Greek. I was overwhelmed and replied, "No, but I know a little Latin." He talked rapidly, forcefully, about his research. Then, abruptly, he held up his notepapers, shook them, and said passionately, "You must understand: the whole world runs to my schedule!"

He meant it!

The scene is indelible and one of the highlights of my life.

As a third analysis, Arnold J. Toynbee offers observations in *A Study of History*, (1947). The plan of his study includes the genesis, growth, and breakdown of civilizations. He touches on churches; heroic ages; contrasts between civilizations; rhythms in histories; the prospect of Western Civilization; and inspirations of histories.

Toynbee's research led to his inclusion and systemic comparison of 22 societies. The list reveals the immensity of the research task: Western, Christian, Orthodox-Byzantine, Iranian, Arabic, Islamic, Hindu, Far Eastern Chinese, Far

Eastern Korean-Japanese, Hellenic, Egyptian, Andean, Mexican, Yucatan, and Mayan.

Of special significance to this brief commentary on the Iraq Mesopotamian Fertile Crescent is the careful consideration by Toynbee of the concept of a universal church. The universal church of the Universal Islamic State is, of course, Islam itself.

"Broadly speaking," Toynbee wrote, "Christianity is a universal church originating in a germ that was alien to the society in which it played a part, while Islam originated in an autumn that was indigenous."

The Indic Society (Hindu) embraced, as its universal church Hinduism; Sinic society in the Far East looked to Confucius; and Lao-Tze Egypt accepted the religion of Osiris and the monumental *Book of the Dead*.

As to the western hemisphere's North American, Meso - American and South American societies, cultures, and civilizations: Mayan, Yucatan, Andean, and Mexican – Toynbee's studies indicate these to be recognizable only in ruins of temples, irrigation projects, and roadways.

These three monumental studies cast light upon a world view of ancient Mesopotamia, Babylon, the Tigris Euphrates cultures, and the Fertile Crescent of Iraq.

3

Egypt's Pharaonic Nile River

Concerning Egypt, I will now speak at length because nowhere are there so marvelous things, not in the whole world are there to be seen so many works of unspeakable greatness
— *Herodotus*

Herodotus, noted Greek "Father of History," marveled at the cultures and civilization along the northern 4175 miles of Africa's Nile River.

Alexandria, once called El Iskandariya, was once a dominant seaport noted for its white marble 400-foot-high Lighthouse — one of the Seven Wonders of the ancient world. From there to a point some 400 miles southward to what is the present-day area of the Aswan High Dam, Lake Nasser and the Sudan - United Arab Republic boarder, the Nile has been the liquid lifeline for millions of persons, hundreds of communities, towns, and cities. From there emerged dozens of cultures and a magnificent Mother Civilization.

Egyptian beginnings, established at a time before 3100 BC at Marimda Banī Salāma, a Neolithic Delta community between 5000 and 4000 BC, included both hunters and nomads from Libyan, Nubian, Western Asian areas that merged into communities or city-states with consequent major governments. Represented were lower or northern Egypt, and upper or southern Egypt. Confusion over the terms "upper" and "lower" may exist when looking at north-oriented maps. Remember that the Nile River flows northwardly, unlike – for example – the Mississippi River, which flows southwardly.

United Egypt's cultural history may be viewed along the timeline:

1   Dynastic Period: 3050 BC
2   Age of the Pyramids: 2686 BC
3   Empire Age - Middle Kingdom: 2040 BC
4   Decline of Empire: 1070

The Decline of Empire period witnessed the Greek pre-emptive invasion by Alexander the Great in 332 BC

From the historian's perspective, Egypt faded from European view. It was as if a great silence engulfed Egypt's Majestic Nile Valley for some two thousand years.

Not until 1790 AD did a stunning archaeological miracle occur. The resurrection of Egypt stemmed from three conjunctive events: the invasion of Egypt by France under Napoleon Bonaparte in 1790, the discovery by the French of a black granite slab in the fields of Rashid (Rosetta), and the deciphering of the Rosetta Stone writings, including the three contained scripts: Hieroglyphic, Demotic, and Greek. The translation was accomplished in 1832 by Jean Champollion, one of the many savants assisting Napoleon's explorative efforts.

Suddenly, Europeans become aware: through writings, sketches, paintings of artists, scholars, archaeologists who were excitedly compiling data about ancient Egypt and detailing the almost unbelievable achievements in colossal monuments; the Nile Valley and the Egyptian world became the center of worldwide attention and fascination.

The great monuments of the Pharaonic Period were instant attractions. The Step Pyramid at Saggara, constructed about 2650 BC, is considered to be the oldest free-standing stone structure in the world. Giza's Great Pyramid of Cheops, Chephren, and Mycerinus is a spectacle that includes the huge, inscrutable Sphinx. Other wonders commanding European attention included the Valley of Remises, the Colossi of Menon, the Temples of Amun, Mut, and Amenhotep at Luxor and Karnak.

True, much of this mighty civilization is lost, buried in desert sands, vandalized and looted by treasure hunters, and ravaged by waves of military antagonists. Additionally, many tombs, monuments, and cities were inundated by the Aswan Dam project of 1902. It must be emphasized, however, that some 40 teams of archaeologists from nations around the world assisted in removing and saving treasures from the inundating waters of the Nile.

The achievement of the dam project, including the reservoir and its irrigation and hydroelectric system, offers its own defense to the undeniable charge that some 100 miles of Egyptian – Sudanese - Nubian Nile River territory is now protectively managed. The system assists in the control of the annual flooding that occurs from June to October. The two-mile-long, one billion-dollar project provides water storage for the irrigation of twp million acres within the vast desert area. The hydroelectric system provides much-needed energy for the heavily populated Nile Valley area.

Many publications by French savants, scientists, artists, and archaeologists opened the eyes of the modern world. Resulting works included the multiple-volume *Description de l' Egypt* by Dominique Dinon (1808-1828), *Voyage dans la Basse a la Haute,* also by Dinon, *Precis du Systeme Hiroglyphique* by Champollion, *Travel Journal of the 1828-29 Franco Tuscan Expedition in Egypt,* by Ippolito Rosellini, regarded as the father of Italian Egyptology.

The stunning beauty of Pharaonic Egyptian temples, and the megaliths, monuments, writings, and ornamentation, is wonderfully captured by Catharine Roehrig in her work *Ancient Egypt: Artists and Explorers in the land of the Pharaohs* (2003), which describes the evocation of millennial history by names like Memphis, Giza, Saggare, Medinet Harbur and Mit Raluna."

In a magnificent summary statement – a veritable rubric of the basics of civilization – National Geographic Society editors described the development of history's tools as the heart of Egypt's Nile Valley Civilization as a "simple astronomy, an accurate calendar, a written language, an accounting system, and basic construction devices."

To the insightful outline of history's tools must be added the underlying matrix of purpose and passion, the energy-motivation that fuels all cultures and civilizations. This energy is created, nurtured, expressed, and sometimes enforced, through spirit structure and revealed by a consensus of faith and formalized as a religious world view. It is necessary to recognize that the Western European - American inheritance and understanding of history and religions has been generally confined to the mythology of ancient Greece and Rome, as well as the bibliography of the Judeo-Christian world view.

The home of Greek Gods was Mount Olympus. Zeus was Father of the Gods. Names in the Greek Pantheon, such as Poseidon, Aphrodite, Eros, Athena, and Hermes are well known. The Romans accepted that same mythological universe and added their spirit gods: Juno, Mars, Cupid, Venus, Minerva, Mercury, Bacchus, and Saturn, along with Terminus (Landmarks), Pomona (Fruit), Flora (Flower Goddess), et al.

Lares and Penates were the everyday protectors of family life and households. Western European - American recognition of religions representing other ancient cultures and civilizations presents a far different – and sometimes indifferent – perspective of acceptance. Examples include the religion of ancient Persia (Zend-Avesta, the exposition of the Zoroastrian world view described in the Veda four *Books of Wisdom*), including the dualism of cosmic Good Spirits (Ahura Mazda) and Evil Spirits (Angra Mainyo).

Other examples include India's world of Buddhism (Buddha: the Enlightened One, a religious teacher circa sixth century BC; life produces suffering; extreme felicity (Nirvana) and ultimate goal), and China's Lao-Tze (600 BC), reputed Founder of Taoism (Tao: the way; opponent of stage government; advocate of small, peaceful communities).

As discussed hereinbefore, the Civilization of Pharaonic Egypt received little attention until Napoleon's arrival on the stage in 1790, leading to the introduction of Egypt to the world in the 1800's.

Compared to our acceptance of Greek and Roman mythology, Western European - American attention and understanding has not been extended to the magnificent ancient civilizations of the East, nor to those of the Western Hemisphere, e.g., Mayan, Toltec, Aztec, and Incan). The mass and magnificence of Khufu's Pyramid has caught our attention and respect. The 2.5 million massive building stones averaged 2.25 tons, rising more than 481 feet and dominating desert sands for millennia. They represented deathlessness and protected an individual's spirit. This we can grasp and respect. We lose the significance, however, of the countless details and major historical events.

Perhaps the most unusual figure in Pharaonic history was Ikhnaton, the Heretic King. It was he who voiced for his people the first official expression of Monotheism. Ikhnaton expressed, formalized, and enforced the concept throughout Egypt. It is fascinating to reflect upon the result. At his death, the populace and officialdom returned to a polytheistic world-view

.

4

Indigenous Peoples

Can my sorrow ever be appeased while we are divided by the mighty seas? It is a vast and watery road over which I look toward the horizon. My daughter, O my daughter"
   – *Easter Island Tablet*

Easter Island, known among the Polynesians as Rapa Nui, is often called the loneliest place on earth. It is a tiny island in the vast waters of the Pacific Ocean, some 2,300 miles distant from the government of Chile which has ruled the island since 1888. The Admiral who "discovered" Rapa Nui forced its native king to sign a treaty with Chile.

Currently, the native population of some 2500 persons is wrestling with a three-fold survival problem. As the island's only town, Hanga Roa is burdened with tourists who come to see the world-famous gigantic statues, governance is remote and indifferent, and – above all – these Pacific islanders want to save their native culture.

To address these challenges, the self-appointed members of the Rapa Nui Parliament are trying to have the island's colonial status reviewed by Chile and the United Nations in an effort to achieve self-rule. The indigenous Easter Island people want to preserve their culture, including the language, customs, and history. The new world represented by Chile, with its Spanish language, television, and tourists, is threatening to drown the conflicted culture of these Islanders, and threatening to erase a millennium-long memory about their leader. Hotu Matu, who arrived with a small crew of Polynesians and established Rapa Nui, established a culture which, today, can and should be preserved as these islanders visualize it.

The great haunting sculptures, along with the mystery of the island's bird culture and the rich language of Polynesia, undoubtedly prompted author Will Durant to comment in his work *Story of Civilization*, that the gigantic statuary of Easter Island "indicate a glory departed, a people not rising to civilization but fallen from high estate."

Many indigenous peoples in today's world, including those found in Australia, Bolivia, Canada, Ecuador, Guatemala, Hawaii, India, Mexico, New Zealand, Peru, Russia, and the United States, are confronted with the daunting challenge of rescuing or preserving their past. It is not easy to exist as the sub-entity, a putative inferior in a seemingly harsh and indifferent world. Such scenarios are illustrated in the struggles of the sixth largest economic structure in the world: California, USA.

In 1848, California's indigenous population was about 150,000. By 1860, only some 30,000 Indians remained, most without land rights. California's "Indians," according to Prof. Carol Goldberg, Director of Law and American Indian Studies at UCLA, "were hunted like game animals during the first decades of statehood, and thousands were killed. The State's first Governor, Peter Burnett, famously declared that 'a war of extermination will continue to be waged' between the races" until the Indian race becomes extinct.

The genocidal attitude of the "superior white man" has been described by a Native American as one which included estimates of the number of indigenous people living in America before the arrival of the Europeans "as high as 10 million." By the end of the Great Plains wars in the 1890's," wrote Jasmine Cloud, of New York's Seneca Nation, "our numbers were reduced to 250,000. The systematic elimination of a race through conventional and biological warfare, mass murder, hybridization and dispossession of land continues to cast a very dark shadow over the prospects for Native Americans."

A most devastating revelation of the U.S. Government's formal antipathy towards indigenous peoples occurred between 1810 and 1836 in the State of Georgia. In the Treaty of Hopewell, the new nation of the United States of America and the Cherokee Nation foreswore conflict for a guarantee that Native American territory would be inviolate.

By 1810, the Cherokee had discarded their old system of Justice, obliterated all outstanding crimes, set up a completely new cultural discipline, a police force, as well as circuit, district and a Supreme Court. A Cherokee Independence Day was celebrated in 1827, announcing a new governmental structure that was supported by a written constitution that described the new republic as "one of sovereign and independent nations of the world."

Gold was discovered in Georgia in 1828. The state, by statute, declared all Cherokee laws and treaties to be null and void. In 1810, a bill for removal of the Cherokee Nation to the west was placed before the U.S. Congress. There was but one southern vote opposing the bill, that of Congressman David Crockett. The bill passed. Crockett lost in the next election.

By 1836, the deadly government-forced march took place, enforced by U.S. troops. Hundreds died on what became known as the Cherokee Trail of Tears. The takeover of Cherokee lands via broken treaty, legal and political pronouncement, and military force has dominated and motivated the suppression of the indigenous peoples of the United States. A curious extension of this suppressive domination is illustrated by Hawaii's experience. One has but to read Queen Liliuokalani's appeal to the U.S. to intercede on her behalf after a group of businessmen (aided by the US Navy) deposed her and formed a new provisional government for the Hawaiian Islands.

"I do earnestly and respectfully protest," she wrote, "against the assertion of ownership by the United States of America of the so-called Crown Lands amounting to about one million acres and which are my property."

The brilliant young Frenchman Alexis de Tocqueville, may have best described the U.S. national character (and his own) when he concluded that "while the savages were endeavoring to civilize themselves, the Europeans continued to surround them, on every side, and to confine them within narrow limits. "The Indians have been ruined by a competition which they had not the means of sustaining," wrote de Tocqueville. "They were isolated in their own country and their race only constituted a little colony of troublesome strangers in the midst of a numerous and dominant people."

It has been much the same in Australia, where settlers – many of them outcasts from England – arrived in 1778. They found vast lands occupied by a people who had no visible governmental structure, no clear evidence of land ownership. Indeed, Australia was *Terra Nullius* to the newcomers, a land without people.

"If the aborigines fought back, they were killed," wrote Barbara Bedr. "If they got in the way, they were moved from their ancestral land."

Alexis de Tocqueville would have understood the problem and the harsh solutions employed; a truth so hard to admit and, in contrition, so hard to remedy.

On May 28, 2000, Australia's prime minister refused to issue an apology to the aboriginal populace for "inappropriate conduct" exhibited by his country in the past. The issue came up on the occasion of the 2000 Olympic Games and the controversy over the selection of athlete Cathy Freeman, who was chosen to carry the Olympic torch. Some 200,000 Australians walked across Sydney's Great Harbor Bridge in support of reconciliation with Australia's aboriginal people.

Above the marchers, an airplane skywriter towed a banner with a compassionate message in vast letters: SORRY.

Somewhere, the Australian national anthem was playing:

For those who come across the seas
We've boundless plains to share;
With courage let us all combine
To advance Australia Fair.

Considering the problems confronting indigenous peoples world-wide, brings the realization that the Statue of Liberty (the U.S. monument formally known as "Liberty Enlightening the World") has an unexpected hidden message to convey. Recall that portion of the message engraved on the pedestal below the statue is a poem written by Emma Lazarus:

Give me your tired, your poor
Your huddled masses yearning to be free.
The wretched refuse of your teeming shore.
Send these, the homeless, tempest-tossed to me,
I lift my lamp beside the Golden Door.

What is hidden by silence in that beautiful message (just as it is hidden Australia's Anthem)? Not expressed, but left out? The answer: Everybody's Welcome – except those who were there first. The indigenous: Australia's Aborigines and the Native Americans of the United States. These are the people who don't have to be counted or included, who don't warrant a "lamp beside the Golden Door."

Fortunately, issues of justice, legal rights, and equity have come to the forefront on the world stage of globalization. Concepts of respect and equality are being openly expressed, expected and – in some cases – enforced. The new world order includes indigenous peoples. There is a new magic and vigor in the assertion that "all men are created equal, that they are endowed by their creator with certain unalienable Rights, that among these are Life, Liberty and the pursuit of Happiness."

The Maoris of New Zealand have achieved substantial, well-deserved recognition of tribal rights, real estate ownership and voting rights.

In Canada, the Inuit People, once commonly identified as Eskimos, have finally achieved notion status with the generous cooperation of the government. Approximately one-fifth of Canadian territory has been formally dedicated to the new Inuit government. For the first time in their history, the indigenous people have their own homeland and government, structured within the family of nations. There is a new nation on the world stage; it is called Nunavut, or "Our Land!"

In the United States, a federal judge has ordered the U. S. Bureau of Indian Affairs to cease destroying thousands of files documenting disposition of Native American monies "held in trust. The case involves all Indian Nations located west of the Mississippi and examines charges of gross mismanagement of millions of dollars held in trust for some 300,000 Native Americans. It is the largest class action suit against the government in history.

A "Declaration of Indigenous Peoples Rights" was prepared in 2000 by the United Nations as a commitment to indigenous peoples worldwide.

The "Mexica Movement" is a group created in 1993 to encourage understanding of the significance of Indian cultures, including civilizations inhabiting Mexico prior to the arrival of Spanish invaders. One Mexica leader, describing cultural confrontation, observed: "There is a lot of shame. Our people associate being indigenous with being poor, being illiterate, being at the bottom."

It is to the issue of being "at the bottom" that some 150 world leaders gathered at the Millennium Summit in New

York City in September 2000. Two major "global targets" intended to "halve extreme poverty by 2015" and "ensure globalization leaves none behind."

It is reassuring to see in the "Declaration of Rights of Indigenous Peoples" intent to insure that "indigenous peoples have the right to the full and effective enjoyment of all human rights and fundamental freedoms recognized in the Charter of the United Nations, the Universal Declaration of Human and International Human Rights and International Human Rights Law."

Consider the community of yesteryear, today and tomorrow, a little-known indigenous island of some 5500 residents located on 490 acres in the heart of the sprawling metroplex of Phoenix, Arizona. Formerly known as "Yaqui Town," it is now the town of Guadalupe. The unique nature of this community was recognized by President Woodrow Wilson in 1915 by the establishment of a 40-acre site dubbed La Quarenta" to be a trust land for Yaqui peoples. The lands were extended through donations.

The Yaqui Indians of the Sonoran Desert were caught up in the tragic diaspora of 1887, in which flight from northern Mexico was the only alternative to slavery or extermination by a genocidal Mexican government. As a result, Yaquis fled from villages located along the Sea of Cortes and the U.S. - Mexican borders at Nogales and Obregon, seeking refuge in southern Arizona, especially in the Tucson and Phoenix areas. Fortunately, according to Leah S. Glasser, writing in *Guadalupe's Buried Past*, the Yaqui were recognized by the U.S. Government as political refugees, not as an Indian tribe, so no steps could be taken to settle them on a reservation.

What can be seen in the town of Guadalupe? Some 5000 residents living in very modest homes, many with outdoor family shrines known as Santitos that honor holy figures – all located on 490 acres. The heart of the town is graced by a beautiful church, Our Lady of Guadalupe Parish, which faces a huge open public square. Although incorporated in 1975, new civic buildings have since been constructed. The well-used library has been moved into new quarters. One of its most interesting features is an eight by fourteen foot mural funded by the Arizona Committee of the Arts, depicting *el Dia de Los Muertos*, or "the Day of the Dead."

"There is hope for something better," stated a Yaqui resident, "but there is also contentment with something less, so long as family and friends and old familiar customs provide a sense of security and comfort."

On the roadway entrance to Guadalupe there is a central monument called *Pico*, a small pyramidal structure topped by a cross. The monument displays writing in English on one side and Yaqui on the other, naming veterans who served in WWII, Korean Conflict, and the Vietnam Conflict.

Descendants of the Yaqui diaspora have fled one homeland and have found and established another, and are contributing in worthy and honorable fashion to both old and new ways of life in their community.

Government relationships with indigenous people can be viewed from contrasting perspectives.

In Virginia, British colonials first arrived in 1607. They landed at a place they called Jamestown, where they were met by some 3,500 Chickahominy, Monacan, Nansemond, and Rappahannock.

Of the 562 federally "recognized" tribes, the Jamestown area natives were never included, since agreements reached between these tribes and the British Government were never formally recognized by the United States. It created a problem that became even larger than the Great Dismal Swamp, an area south of Norfolk, Portsmouth, and Chesapeake, Virginia.

The Virginia state government essentially legislated the Indian race out of existence in 1924 during the nationwide embrace of the disastrous "eugenics movement" which advocated – among other concepts – the preservation of white supremacy by prohibiting racial intermarriage, when it passed the Racial Integrity Act which classified racial categories as "white" and "colored."

The U.S. Bureau of Indian Affairs requires documentation that a tribe has been in continuous existence since 1900 and since the Bureau's "official paperwork" had expunged the tribes' racial identity, no "proof" existed! It has been a long, tormented, and uphill climb for Native Americans.

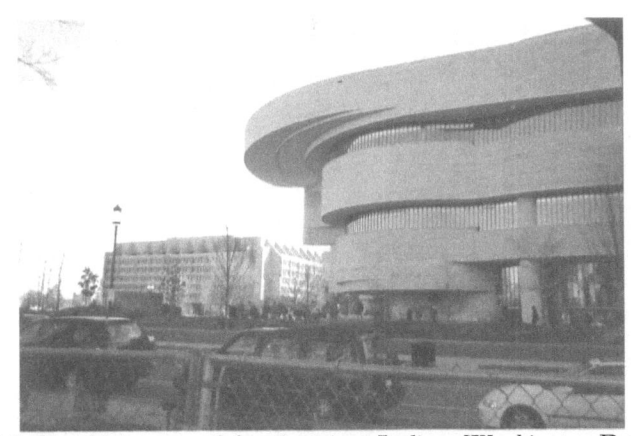

National Museum of the American Indian, Washington D.C.

Ultimately, individuals with 1/16th Native American ancestry were exempted from classification as "Colored." In 1967, the Supreme Court struck down the Racial Integrity Act. In 1997, the Virginia General Assembly formally apologized for the for the 1924 law, offering to pay for "Indians" to have the race on their birth certificates corrected."

Action is being taken by the U.S. Congress to grant federal recognition to the Jamestown tribes, with support from the National Congress of Americans and coordinators of the Jamestown Commemoration.

In 2004, a new national museum opened with an official "Message of Welcome," delivered by W. Richard West, Jr., a Southern Cheyenne, and director of the National Museum of the American Indian.

The time was 1:35 PM, on Wednesday, September 22, 2004. Some 25,000 Native Americans from the entire

American continent gathered with the Smithsonian "family" to celebrate "Dedication and Reconciliation." The Museum, a $210 million structure, is located on the last planned spot on the Mall. The days-long festivities were attended by an estimated 80,000 persons who relished such declarations as 'Welcome to North America" and "Welcome Home." Hundreds of school children on local and distant field trips and interested in Native American history were among the marchers and spectators enjoying the collage of cultures.

5

Acronyms of Power: MAD, SAD, NMD

Even in war moral power is to physical as three parts out of four.
— Napoleon Bonaparte III

June 17, 1574, is the putative date that England's Francis Drake anchored his ship the *Golden Hind* in a bay on the west coast of the "New World." The bay, now named for the navigator, is located a short distance north of San Francisco.

Drake played the role of the powerful acquisitor to the fullest extent, a quality spoofed in an archeological hoax that survived some forty years. The explorer was purported to have inscribed on a "plate of brasse" his declaration unto all men that he had taken possession "of this kingdome whose king and people freely resigne their right and title in the whole land unto Her Maiestiees keeping." In the hoax, Drake then named the territory *Nova Albion*, a literary representation of New Britain.

The "Plate of Brass" was sealed with a sixpence as part of the hoax by a playful fraternity of California history buffs, hidden in 1933, and "discovered" in 1936 in Marin County,

California. Acquired in 1937 by the University of California
Berkeley, the object was displayed in the Bancroft Library
until 2005, years after the hoax was detailed by four
researchers. Edward Von der Porten, Raymond Aker, Robert
W. Allen, and James M. Spitze published the account of their
findings in *California History* in 2002.

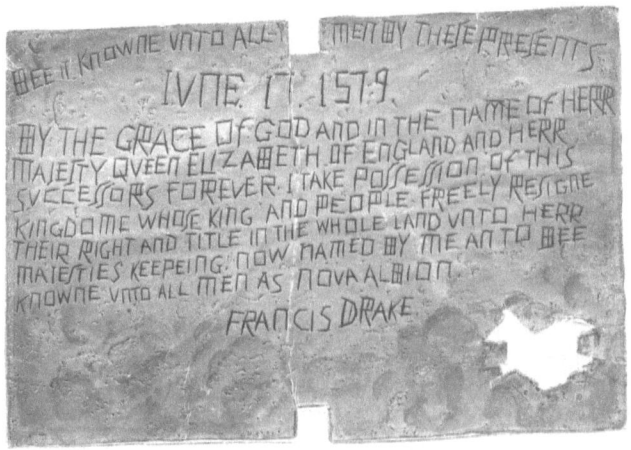

The Purported Brass Plate of Francis Drake

   Perhaps the difficulty in earlier attempts to debunk the
hoax, which was questioned by experts from the start, is its
reflection of the general perception of the free-booting,
conquering, take-over attitudes of the Western hemisphere's
newcomers. Authors of the text inscribed on the "Brass
Plate" and attributed to Drake recalled the pillaging attitudes
and philosophies of explorers of the 15th, 16th, and 17th
centuries. The grasping avariciousness that motivated soldiers
of fortune was often accompanied or protected by the
prophylactic adjurations of religion.

   The invasions that led to the domination, devastation, and
eventual extermination of cultures in Mexico and Peru are
examples. As described in Oswald's Spengler's *Decline of the
West,* the Aztec civilization of Mexico "was not starved,
suppressed or thwarted, but murdered in the full glory of it

unfolding, destroyed like a sunflower whose head is struck off by one passing." This American Indian civilization, wrote Spengler, "with an extent and resources far superior to those of the Greek and Roman states of Hannibal's day" had a carefully ordered financial system, a highly developed legislature, and a wealth of literature in several languages "that was washed out by a handful of bandits in a few years."

Of the great city of Tenochtitlan not a stone remains above ground.

The argument for "Stupidity on Stilts" can be well-advanced by the consideration of an astounding historical event. The construction of the "Maginot Line" by the French was a defensive fortification created at enormous expense, stretching along the French-German border.

The boundary was named for Andre Maginot, the French Minister of War and World War I hero who was severely wounded in combat. The elaborate network of bunkers was buttressed by massive concrete supports and stretched some 150 miles. The complex contained living quarters and an underground railroad, and stocked heavy artillery. It was described by awe-stricken observers as an impregnable fortress with the conveniences of a modern city.

Considered a marvel of publicly-displayed defensive military strength, the line was the symbol of security. It represented the mindset of the era, and passionately embraced a triad concept of defense, security, and power. This concept was also embraced and expressed in the Stalin line of Russia, Germany's Siegfried Line (a relevant derivation from Old High German, *sigu* = victory + *fridu* = peace), and the Great Coast Defense Fortress of Singapore.

The Maginot Line did not extend to the Franco-Belgium border, however. In World War II, German troops simply outflanked the exposed Maginot by invading from Belgium in the north, down and behind the French fortress made useless by the simple expedient of going around its exposed end.

Singapore's Great Fortress was similarly circumvented since the huge 16-inch guns of the fort could only fire seaward. The invading Japanese went north and marched down from the landward side!

"Stupidity on Stilts" may be difficult to appreciate – or perhaps not – but, whether delusional, insane, or pragmatically unavoidable, the following data are revelatory and the stuff of nightmares. Welcome to the world of MAD SAD NMD!

We lived in the Cold War era for decades during a face-off with the U.S.S.R, behind the security policy called MAD, for Mutually Assured Destruction." It worked. Now, as the U.S. emerges as the major military, economic, and nuclear World Power, a new Threat emerges as rogue nations, movements, groups, and individuals are named, publically identified and charged by the United States. At this juncture, the U.S. announces it is time for SAD (Self Assured Destruction) to serve as the great deterrent.

SAD is a belief that any nation that permits a nuclear device to be launched from its territory against another country will see its capitol city removed from the face of the earth.

The policy would be supported by a new United States National Missile Defense (NMD) system. Initial cost: estimated between $33 billion and $180 billion.

This new system disregards the U.S. agreement covering the 1972 Anti-Ballistic Missile Treaty and waves aside the recent failures of two highly publicized tests of the ratification of the Comprehensive Nuclear Test Ban Treaty (CNTBT).

Adverse reaction to the U.S. NMD program was expressed clearly by Russian Federation President Vladimir Putin, who issued a warning on June 27, 2000.

"Either we will be able to save and enhance by joint effort everything we achieved towards non-proliferation or reduction of nuclear weapons," said Putin, "or the entire system of international and bilateral agreements developed in past years will be threatened."

In addition to Russia, China and North Korea have been particularly critical of the U.S. as voiced by China's chief arms control negotiator, who concluded that "such plans could touch off an arms race and upset the delicate global strategic balance.

The development of NMD is tantamount to drinking poison to quench thirst." All of these MAD-SAD-NMD protective warning and security systems are a far cry from the earlier U.S. deployed surface-to-air missiles dating from the 1950s. Ajax and Hercules (both mythological Greek heroes of great strength and courage) were located in 211 sites throughout the United States. Los Angeles County began demolishing its 16 sites in the year 2000, southern California sites euphemistically called "the Ring of Supersonic Steel" guarding the L.A. Basin from anticipated bomber attacks.

A nightmarish picture presented in the year 2000 on a segment of the CBS program *60 Minutes* described the unique, little-known groups of highly-trained military technologists. One group was located in Russia, the other somewhere in the U.S. They are the "Missileries."

Each group is now – as they have been for years – on 24-hour alert. Each group monitors electronic consoles capable of launching a nuclear warhead missile response within seconds. Each warhead is backed by a national stockpile of some 6000 warheads. Each warhead is 20 times more powerful than the bomb that devastated Hiroshima. Efforts were successfully made in subsequent years to share military missile information between Russian and the U.S. in an effort to build a bridge of national rapprochement. Those efforts have since ceased. Confrontational readiness is back to square one, based in the calculus of 24/7/365.

One must acknowledge, understand, and accept the mania of domination, the worldwide indifference to the rights of indigenous peoples, the reality of preemptive military aggression, and the fearful defensive need for security.

The United States, as the acknowledged major worldwide superpower, has established the first global security system in history. U.S. military garrisons now encircle the globe. Bases are located on all continents, excepting Antarctica. The U.S.

Defense Department's Base Structure Report lists 702 overseas facilities in some 130 countries. 6000 bases in the U.S. and its territories are staffed by more than 253,000 military personnel, and a similar number of U.S. civilians plus some 45,000 foreign employees. Our bases are served by the military Mobility Command, including some 71 Learjets.

Austin Chalmers Johnson wrote in *The Sorrows of Empire; Militarism, Secrecy, and the End of the Republic* that "once upon a time, you could trace the spread of imperialism by counting up a country's colonies." Johnson asserts that America's version of the colony is the modern military base, which does a good job of covering what might be called the 'arc of instability.' He identified the area as extending from the Andean region of South America – ostensibly Columbia – through North Africa, then sweeping across the Middle East to the Philippines and Indonesia.

The system is designed to permit the U.S. to maintain a global presence to quickly confront and contest critical situations worldwide. The bases – sometime termed "lily pads" - are for jumping from one crisis to another.

Johnson maintains the war on terrorism is only a small part of the base strategy, and that "the real reason for construction this new ring of U.S. bases along the equator is to expand our empire and reinforce our military domination of the world."

In January 2004, a $1.5 billion donation to the Salvation Army was announced by the estate of the late Joan Kroc, widow of McDonald's founder Ray Kroc. She was known for donations of hundreds of millions of dollars to promote world-wide programs assisting education, health care, African famine relief, the Arts, and the encouragement of peace and nuclear non-proliferation efforts.

The Salvation Army was organized in 1870 to provide "soup, soap and salvation" for lost souls, and now manages soup kitchens, rehabilitation centers, thrift stores, medical facilities, group homes, disaster relief efforts, and related services in some 100 countries. More than 60 million meals are served and 10 million lodging nights are made available to the needy annually. The Salvation Army has made remarkable changes from the approach adopted by co-founder William Booth, who brought "religion to the poor."

Philanthropist Kroc and the Salvation Army represent a world view that is dedicated to service, compassionate activism, rehabilitation of the needy, and peaceful survival. There are no Maginot Lines constructed to defend their vision. There are two fundamental philosophies involved: *Ducunt Fata volentem, nolentem trahunt* (Fate leads the willing, drags the unwilling) and *Benedictus qui venit in nomine Domini* (Blessed are those who come in the name of the Lord).

These philosophies are based upon, and owe their existence to: *Coqito, Ergo Sum* (I think, therefor I am), *Deusest* (God exists), *Corpore sunt* (Bodies exist), as expressed by the French philosopher René Descartes.

6

Alternative Methods for Dispute Resolution

A physical law tells us that every structure has its limits beyond which it cannot be extended without endangering its cohesion ad functioning unity, Galileo remarked that a giant with the same proportion as an ordinary man...experiencing an inordinate increase in height, would fall and be crushed under his own weight.
– György Kepes, Hungarian-born artist and art theorist

I t is not news that the U.S. is a singularly litigious society, nor is it news that we share a tenuous global lead in the number of persons housed within our prison systems. It is newsworthy that our national addiction to litigation produced during the past decade some 15,000,000 lawsuits, some 800,000 attorneys, 17,000 courthouses; some $16 billion in awards, and another $19 billion in expenses.

As an attorney, I am painfully aware of former U.S. Supreme Court Justice Warren Burger's 1973 statement that indicated he accepted as a working hypothesis that "one third of the lawyers who appear in serious cases are not really qualified to render fully adequate representation." Nor has the passage of time encouraged a more optimistic hypothesis. Consider this: A federal district judge overturned the death penalty of a Texas inmate, holding that reversal should be made automatic when the defendant's lawyer sleeps during the trial. The U.S. Fifth Circuit Court of Appeals disagreed, and ruled it impossible to determine beyond speculation that the sleeping attorney hurt the defendant's case.

Just as Tevye explained in the 1964 Broadway play, "Every one of us is a fiddler on the roof trying to scratch out a pleasant simple tune" and trying to keep our balance, so – in the professional world of dispute resolution – there is a balance paradigm that includes negotiation, mediation, arbitration, and litigation. A simple sketch has often been employed to illustrate the basic distinction which separates these major dispute resolution procedures: negotiation, arbitration, mediation, and litigation.

What is the substantive issue which divides these four categories? The basic issue is control. Both negotiation and mediation essentially leave the power, control, and the decision in the hands of the disputants. Arbitration and litigation generally transfer the disputant's possession of power and control and eventual decision to a third party or court.

How does our culture cope with the avalanche of contentions? Are there guidelines, mechanisms, and ideas that contribute to dispute diminution, resolution, consensus, and settlement?

Negotiation and mediation guidelines are plentiful, and are found in such works as *Getting To Yes: Negotiating Agreements Without Giving In,* by Roger Fisher and William Fry; *Community Mediation*, edited by Karan Duffy, James Groach, and Paul Olczak; *Basic Mediation Training,* a 40-hour course employed in 2000 by the Kerrville, Texas, Hill Country Alternative Dispute Resolution Center and facilitated by Nancy Wise and Dexter MacBride under Executive Director Mimi Brinker. That program's training manual incorporates information from *The Mediator's Handbook* by Jennifer Beer and Eileen

Stief, which stems from Quaker concepts in determining the "sense of the meeting."

Additionally, there are numerous conferences and seminars presented nationwide that respond to the need for information and training in Alternate Dispute Resolution (ADR).

Prominent among these are those sponsored by the American Bar Association and the Society of Professionals in Dispute Resolution (SPIDR).

Thoughtful practitioners will give careful attention to the following alternative concepts which address ADR Solutions.

The ombudsman concept likely originated in 13th century Sweden despite certain similarities to 3rd century Chinese Yuan, the Roman Tribune, and the 17th century American colonies' Censors. The Ombudsperson may be defined as "one who represents someone" – an agent, representative, or guardian of the peoples' rights.

Amparo is the Mexican adaptation with a unique origin (and a literal Spanish translation of the English term protection). The modern concept, introduced in 1836 by French author and philosopher de Tocqueville in his commentary on the United States Government entitled "Democracy in America," was translated into Spanish and exists by virtue of constitutional incorporation as a vital part of Mexican governmental process.

California's experience with the Spanish *Alcalde* concept was inherent in its early Pueblo days, when the *Alcalde* was not only the leading citizen, but also the chief magistrate with the responsibility of counsel, conciliation, and arbitration. Strangely, the title *Alcalde* was borrowed from the Moors during their occupation of Spain; the title at that time was *Al-Caid* or town judge.

Native Americans offered fascinating approaches in early-day problem solving. One innovative system involved hearing and adjudicating disputes by non-relatives brought from nearby communities. These adjudicators were called "crossers" for their crossing of the lines of party interests.

To identify processes whereby society preserves freedom and expression, defends private ownership of property, maintains avenues for settlement of disagreement, and provides alternatives for control of controversy, many categories may be studied in analyzing problems. Included are: discussion, negotiation, voting and litigation. Elements also include the press, especially as seen in features such as Op-Ed pages and Letters to the Editor; community meetings (including social, civic, and political); professional association meetings, seminars, and colloquia.

In the 2000 U.S. presidential election the outcome was ultimately settled in the courts, a fact the *Los Angeles Times* declared on November 12th as a "demonstration that both campaigns put their trust in a quintessentially American way of solving arguments: litigation."

As a formal process to clarify, achieve and enforce dispute resolution, litigation represents in a most conclusive way, a method to determine and pronounce what is "right" and what is "wrong."

Truth is the needlepoint on which the entire structure of litigation and justice is supported. The imperative and exactitude of truth-telling is the point on which our whole system is balanced.

"I swear (affirm) to tell the truth, the whole truth and nothing but the truth" is a phrase repeated countless times, often with the hand upon the Holy Bible. Judicial opinions have emphasized that if the truth is not told, then divine judgment is invoked through the Book and the Oath. The very Book upon which the Oath or Affirmation may be predicated contains warnings "Swear not at all" and "If any man sue thee at law and take away thy coat, let him have thy cloak also."

At the Claremont (California) Dispute Resolution Center (CDRC), the question was raised: "Why have so few cities created a city-sponsored mediation center?"

Of some 450 cities and towns, CDRC officials could not name another city-based and city-operated dispute resolution center! Was there no perceived need? Were there no serious neighbor disputes, no landlord-tenant conflicts, no employer-employee confrontations; no unresolved domestic disputes, or no juvenile detentions where restitution concepts might be employed? The group in 1988 encouraged the establishment of a mediation center in the city of Diamond Bar, encouraged community groups to become involved in ADR, and began creation of a volunteer community and city government regional network, with trained volunteer mediators.

A four-corner structure was visualized, but the need for an initiator or administrator to serve as a central, energizing force immediately became apparent, changing the "structure" to five-parted. In the first 8 months, 110 cases were processed with 88 cases successfully settled upon consensus. Case types included landlord-tenant, neighbor disputes, insurance claims, payment defaults, employer-employee, and contract disputes.

City government has formally embraced the concept of volunteerism; consider the committees and commissions that are integral working parts of the machinery of municipal governance.

I am constantly impressed by the diligence and devotion exhibited by my fellow members who have been selected to serve on the City Planning Commission, a non-paying job. We are essentially volunteers, as are the equally skilled, equally diligent members of the Parks and Recreation Commission, the Traffic and Safety Commission, the General Plan Advisory Committee, and the Source Reduction Committee. Considering their salary ($400 monthly), the members of the City Council are volunteers: they serve for indirect rewards which may include personal satisfaction, civic duty fulfillment, or public recognition. The reservoir of mature, experienced volunteers has been a constant in our society.

City government, with so productive a volunteer environment, should take advantage of the public service potential of grass-roots mediation. Encouragement to do so comes from many sources. Consider the declaration of the

American Bar Association, expressed in a 1989 "President's Message" to the membership:

"The justice system in most of our major cities is in crisis. A complex web of factors has made civil litigation far too costly, time-consuming, and uncertain. In this environment, access to justice often is not a reality for anyone: the poor, middle class, wealth, and business alike. Alternate dispute resolution, or ADR, offers great promise for improving access to civil justice."

The Diamond Bar City Mediation Program, a visible, public service oriented, not-for-profit organization, cost that city nothing in budgeted dollars. Use of office space – after regular city business hours – local telephone calls, along with forms and records copying are the city's sole support involvement. The program administrator and staff of on-call mediators are volunteers. Public relations releases are prepared by the administrator, who also maintains community contacts with social clubs and business and professional groups.

The following steps are recommended in creating city-town Alternate Dispute Resolution Mediation Centers:

- Recognize local, grass-root needs for practical alternatives to adversarial litigation.
- Rely upon your City's experience with the power and accomplishments of volunteerism.
- Agree to the use of city office space (after regular working hours) for mediation settlements.
- Consider the adoption, by the city, of a Mediation Clause to be incorporated in City contracts.
- Support the mediation program with appropriate announcements/notices in your city newsletter and other publications.

The attention on environment, structure, definition, and process may suggest that ADR is essentially reactive, that the role in responding or assisting in the solution of problems is similar to that of the fireman – putting out the fire. Indeed, the description of the services rendered by the Diamond Bar Mediation Center seems to support the reactive concept; the disputes were in process when they arrived. Volunteer mediators responded to the calls for assistance reactively and were involved in repairing and mending that would return matters to a desired "before" condition.

There is another, far deferent dimension that must be recognized and appreciated, based upon the premise that a dispute is often the harbinger of hope – a sign that help is needed, a cry that new ways must be taken, that old, worn-out premises must be discarded. Recognition of these concepts reveals the reason for the emergence of disputers.

Currently across the U.S. there is a movement advocating the removal of watercourse dams to restore water quality and preserve natural habitats. In 1999, the Edwards Dam on the Kennebec River in Maine was breached. The river is now successfully restoring itself. Twenty-four dams in other areas have been breached and twenty more are scheduled for the same treatment. Many of the projects have caused major disputes that requiring years of patient negotiation. There are some 2.5 million dams in the U.S., blocking streams and rivers for flood control, irrigation, power, and storage purposes.

Dam breaching has, of course, caused disputes. Negotiators and mediators have been involved, often as active agents. The desire to improve through change, to discharge old ideas and practices, creates a different perspective for persons with dispute resolution expertise.

The Pacific Northwest's Columbia-Snake river preservation issue is an example where dozens of facilitators, mediators, arbitrators, and attorneys took part in a Pepperdine University School of Law summer mediation program. The purpose: to study dispute solutions in areas such as the Pacific northwest's salmon problem. Led by two of the area's premier negotiators who were actively involved in seeking solutions for the issues, participants were informed about the complexity and difficulty of bringing federal, state, regional and Native American governments together in an effort to achieve incremental stages of consensus. The efforts were pro-active; disputation reflected demands for change, innovation and preservation of riparian habitats.

In professional dispute resolution practice, there are challenges to both proactive and reactive responsibilities. The opportunities for service – both public and private – are as great as the desire for improvement, progress, and the pressure of change.

The position of ombudsman has potential for effective public service throughout the United States, especially in California, where it may be best realized in the field of education. Most current collegiate ombudsman program attention appears to be focused on procedural issues such as "breaking in" new administrators, explaining confidentiality parameters, and improving visibility and staff structure. Substantive accomplishment opportunities deserve a wider perspective.

Experience on a community college campus (Board of Trustees, Mt. San Antonio College, single campus; 41,000+ students) not only enriched my life, but also opened my eyes to the need for a special objective service in the ombuds office.

There are 104 community colleges in California, processing more than 1.5 million students annually. The system has been described as the largest public education structure in the world. There is scarcely a handful of community institutions with a full-time, staffed ombuds office.

What an opportunity for statewide introduction of the ombuds concept of service! To grasp such an opportunity, the following four-step program is advocated to energize the giant California community college system and to introduce the ombuds concept:

- Raise current state CC funding from $4700 © to the national average of $6200
- Remove regulations (2000 highest in the nation)
- Employ modified charter school concepts
- Create ombuds programs for community college campuses to stimulate innovation, creativity, and cooperative communication with special reference to major areas of concern, e.g., integrity of academic oversight and student scholastic achievement.

The magnitude and performance impact of this immense community college system has led to a clear conclusion, according to Robert Davis and David Wessel in their work *Prosperity: the Coming Twenty Years Boom.* "Three major factors will produce an era of broadly shared prosperity for the American middle class," write the authors, including "globalization, computers, [and] community colleges."

Given the restraints placed upon this giant California system through inadequate funding and suffocating regulations, it is reported that California's community college superimposed regulations exceed the total of any 10 States in the U.S. It is astonishing this educational mammoth survives. Galileo's observation that a giant, experiencing inordinate increases in weight, may fall and be crushed because of that weight, serves to highlight California's community college problem.

The pragmatics of reality: equitable funding for California community colleges is not in the cards for want of vigorous academic and political leadership. Removal of major diminution of strangling regulations is far off. Allowing the colleges the privilege of charter school concepts and procedures may never be realized. Only the concept of a college campus ombuds office has a fair chance of acceptance. There is an educational world of need for strong, constructive, innovative service; a world of need for professional ombuds on-campus presence.

An ombuds office in each of California's community colleges might well become the center of new creative activity, of innovation, of student-faculty-staff-community interaction and understanding. The educational giant should not be allowed to be crushed under its own weight, not under the weight of regulation, nor under the additional weight of administrative ineptitude, political errors or interference.

7

Mosquitoes and Vector Control

Fresh, potable wataer is Man's greatest friend; his most deadly companion is the mosquito.
    – D. DuPont

In 2003, 46 states along with New York City and the District of Columbia published West Nile Virus (WNV) activity. A total of 45 states plus the District of Columbia have published reports involving 9,122 human cases. Among 9004 cases with available clinical and demographic data, the median age was 47 years, ranging from 1 month to 99 years of age. 4,769 (53%) were in males. There have been a total of 223 published WNV related fatalities with a median age of 77 years.

For about 12 years, I served as a member of the board of trustees representing the City of Diamond Bar, California. I am not qualified in the scientific or technical skills required of staff members; my fields are law, valuation, and education. However, despite my want of scientific expertise, the work of the vector control specialists has been, for me, a source of fascination and admiration.

The mosquito-borne West Nile Virus summary of 2003 tells much about the massive problems facing vector control specialists. For me, the trustee experience created a welcome introduction into the vast world of insects and the challenges of myriad diseases. I have learned much in the fecund province of public service.

Mankind's emergence and existence upon this planetary body – principally covered with water but which we perversely call Earth – has been accompanied by a vast array of neighbors. Plants, animals, fish, birds, and insects all share the air, land, and water.

Whether examined by paleo-anthropologists studying fossils dating millions of years ago or revealed in ancient religious narratives describing heaven and hell, darkness and light, water and earth, herb and fruit, fish and foul, beast and cattle, or male and female, this "becoming" has been accompanied by myriads of global neighbors whose survival abilities are astounding and whose complex inter-relationships with the network of life are essential to the health of this planet.

Many voices join the chorus describing the delicate bio-fabric of interaction. Poets intuit this interaction, and relate them in writings such as the impactful thoughts from Sandburg's "Grass", Wordsworth's "Daffodils", Lowell's "June", Byron's "Apostrophe to the Ocean", Holmes' "Chambered Nautilus", Emerson's "Each and All", and Kilmer's "Trees".

Entomologists study the insect armies which march along with mankind. They are appreciative of the beneficent role played by members of the great hymenopterous family (honey bees) and understand the contribution of detritovores (termites, wood-boring beetles). They know the annoying power of the order anophera (pediculus humanism, corporis), the lice which nearly sent Napoleon's soldiers to their knees.

It remains to the entomologists who specialize in vector control, a realm of pathology focused upon organisms carrying pathogens from one host to another, to comfort mankind's most persistent and deadly foe – the mosquito. One is the common house mosquito (culex pipiens) which is a leading representative of some 2,500 different mosquito species.

To the vector control specialists, the mosquito conjures up disquieting visions of diseases such as malaria, yellow fever, dengue, filariasis, encephalitis, and West Nile virus. Specialists know that millions of people die from malaria annually and that a child infected with malaria dies every twelve seconds.

How to relate the data, how to comprehend interlocking implications? One major resource is a brilliantly written and authoritative book entitled *Mosquito: A Natural History of Our Most Persistent and Deadly Foe*, co-authored by journalist Michael D'Antonio and scientist Andrew Spielman. It contains a natural history of our most persistent and deadly foe.

The insights and perspectives about little-known realities of the insect and animal world are deftly interspersed throughout the chapters of the book. For example, mention is made of the case of howler monkeys living atop tall trees in South America and infected by mosquitoes, literally wiped out by yellow fever. In consequence, the forest becomes strangely silent.

Malaria severely dominated Rome for hundreds of years, causing many Pontiffs to refuse to serve there; Italy was known as the worst malaria-ridden nation in Europe. In Cuba, during the Spanish-American War, less than 400 soldiers died in combat while more than 2000 died of disease.

U.S. experience with the mosquito problem includes New Jersey, where the state's chief entomologist John B. Smith began to wrestle with mosquito problems in 1900. He placed heavy emphasis on the concept of control rather than extermination, a concept central to current management of mosquito problems.

It is important to understand that the relationship of mosquitoes and disease was not known when the French started work on one of the world's greatest engineering projects. Ferdinand de Lesseps began construction of the Panama Canal in 1881. By 1884, more than 1,200 workers had died, and that number that would ultimately swell to some 30,000. It was Walter Reed who understood the reason for the terrible death toll and it was William Gorgas who pushed through the enterprise. Yellow fever and malaria were finally suppressed.

General Douglas McArthur faced the problem in the South Pacific and explained to Dr. Paul Russel that one-third of his men were fighting malaria and one-third were recovering, leaving only a third ready and fit for combat.

Crows are vulnerable to the disease. The common house sparrow had a major role in the transmission process. The sparrow (a disease carrier) is a foreign species and came to America because sparrow lovers in New York wanted to bring the entire bird species characteristic in Shakespeare's England, to New York.

The World Health Organization's efforts to combat the worldwide problem of malaria include special attention directed at tropical countries. Roll Back Malaria (RBM) has as a goal to reduce deaths by 5%. The World Bank, United Nation agencies, and many national governments are participating.

In any overview of vector control missions and programs, mention must be made of the supportive basics of control, disease surveillance and education. This Triad is recognized by groups such as the American Mosquito Control Association. My participation in academic activities had led me to follow closely the educational outreach programs of the Greater Los Angeles County Vector Control District (GLACVCD).

A seminal paper presented by the district manager, Dr. Jack Hazelrigg, at a 1990 Conference sponsored by the Mosquito Control Association of California, proposed a vector control educational community outreach program. In the years that followed, the district acted and built upon the concept, interacting with dozens of K-12 public school districts by teaching vector basics to some 3000 students. This unusual educational activity has been working and thoughtfully debated, monitored, and evaluated by the board and staff members.

GLACVCD is not unaware of its territorial responsibilities: its service area embraces 1,330 sq miles, some 1.07 million assessable parcels, 34 cities plus unincorporated county areas, and an estimated population of 4.5 million persons.

Community response to the Vector Control Education Program has been enthusiastic. Students relate to the information, exhibits, and guidelines. Parents share the interest of their children. Vector Control "musts" such as emptying containers of standing water, installing house window screens, and monitoring swimming pools are remembered and acted upon. Children are persistent and persuasive about their newly-realized responsibilities. Students and parents become health network volunteers, and are of great assistance in the district's vector control efforts.

News spread quickly about the educational program. The district received an $85,000 in-kind donation of a 38-foot recreational vehicle chassis, which was custom-outfitted to support the classroom programs. The vehicle – termed the Mobile Education Unit (MEU) – contained interacting projects of technology-targeted interest, live larval specimens, basic scientific equipment, and special hands-on projects.

The MEU enquiry-based science curriculum conforms to California State Board of Education standards as they relate to science, language arts, and health education. Exploratorium displays include "What's a Vector?" "Not in Your Backyard;" "The World of Insects;" "How Do Insects See?" and "Vectors in the News."

In the first year of the experiment, the program was conducted by special classroom visits. Some 3000 students benefitted, embracing the program and sharing teaching responsibilities. The total cost of the program averaged $15 per student. With the advent of the Mobile Education Unit, transportation, time, participation, and cost horizons changed dramatically.

Annual Perspective

Exploratory Program	Current Program
3,000 students	25,000 - 30,000 students
14 cities visited	34 cities visited
$15 per student	$5 per student
(District cost)	(District Cost)

In terms of community outreach, strengthened community ties, improved inner city youth contracts, parental involvement, and enhanced district visibility, the program has accomplished goals far beyond the most optimistic expectations.

"Your district has managed to involve some 30,000 students and perhaps some 60,000 parents in year-round, practical, vector control activities," noted an observer. "In reality, you've created a volunteer staff of almost unbelievable proportions."

With the emergence of national re-evaluation of waterways in terms of natural values and contribution to the health and welfare of all living things, vector control specialists confront a new challenge: the rising number of projects proposed and designed to re-establish wildlife corridors, especially in densely-populated urbanized areas.

It is relatively easy to cleanse waterways in essentially rural or wilderness areas. The 2004 demolition of Embry Dam on the Rappahannock River in Virginia was alternately appreciated and appalled (cost was the main problem, at $10 million). It is the largest U.S. dam of the roughly 190 dams to have been removed since 1999.

A quite different picture emerges when watercourse evaluation is proposed through the medium of conservancies and supportive environmental groups. The restoration of portions of rivers, wetlands, or riparian habitat located in heavily developed city areas is commendable.

But warning flags should be raised. Rivers, wetlands, and riparian habitats produce mosquitoes. They attract wild birds and migratory fowl that serve as hosts for viruses involved in disease cycles. Encephalitis, WNV and other vector-borne infections are endemic in regions such as southern California.

In such major and understandably desirable projects, the caveat relates to public health. In a 2000 position statement regarding San Gabriel and the Lower Los Angeles River and Mountains Conservancy, GLACVCD has outlined the concern of vector control professionals:

"Natural or reclaimed wetlands and other aquatic projects that benefit or enhance the environment can co-exist with the mandates of public health agencies responsible for controlling mosquitoes and vector-associated diseases. However, that can only be accomplished successfully if considerations are given to minimizing the occurrence of vectors. In addition, a successful conservancy must be funded sufficiently to ensure that mosquitoes and other vectors, and the disease they can transmit, will always be monitored for early detection, thereby enabling preventive measures for potential outbreaks."

If the above caveat is not heeded, the envisioned concept of wildlife corridors such as reclaimed wetlands and riparian parks may be transformed, in reality, into "disease corridors."

The public good is often accompanied by long-term cost. A project that does not incorporate public health into its long-term budget considerations may create a disaster. Public officials would do well to heed the message.

8

The Fibonacci Sequence

His neighbors in Pisa called him Bigallone, "the Blockhead." His real name was Leonardo and he was the son of Bonaccio, a customs official whose name means "Simpleton." Leonardo, the Blockhead, stumbled upon one of the greatest mysteries of the Universe.
    – *William Hoffer, in* Smithsonian Magazine

For many years, the story in *Smithsonian Magazine* (December 1975) has stayed with me: the introductory full-page illustration of a young man, wearing a conical hat with astronomical figures and wielding a giant pen. Nine rabbits peered from above and the number .618034 appeared in the center of the sketch. Below it all was the statement "Leonardo the Blockhead used hypothetical rabbits to produce a mysterious series of numbers!"

It is a delight, thinking about the magical accomplishment. How could the "Blockhead" discover the concept that seashells and galaxies have the same structure and proportions as playing cards and the Greek's Parthenon? How could he imagine a structure having a base ratio of

.168034 and accomplish it all because of immortal, fecund rabbits?

.618034

.618034

.618034

.618034

.618034

.618034

.618034

.618034

.618034

.618034

.618034

.618034

It was easy to accept the story; I wanted to believe it. The descriptive article which followed was skillfully presented, buttressed by a half-page illustration of golden rectangles and golden spirals. The Golden Mean of the Greeks became a stunning reality when presented with the assumed proportions of Egypt's Great Pyramids at Giza.

Reflecting upon my quick acceptance of this wondrous story, I realized I had been conditioned a ling time ago to an equally quick acceptance of success stories depicting struggling youths who later achieved recognition. My early childhood reading included the Horatio Alger Jr. books *Sam's Chance, Sink or Swim, Bound to Rise,* and *Tattered Tim.* I read dozens of these penny novels written by an ordained minister who became involved in the management of the Newsboys' Lodging House in New York City, an organization concerned with assisting foundling and runaway boys. Alger's influence upon youth has been described as powerful and unsurpassed. He was the most popular U.S. author over the last 30 years of the 19th century, authoring some 100 books with publishing totals estimated at some 30,000,000 copies.

In recent years I have learned considerably more about Leonardo Fibonacci and my appreciation of his studies and contributions to Western culture has grown almost to awe.

Italian Leonardo Fibonacci (1180-1250) was also known as Leonardo of Pisa. A mathematician and merchant, he has been described as the most original and capable mathematician of the medieval Christian world, perhaps of the entire Middle Ages. The mathematical renaissance in the west begins with him.

Four books are attributed to Leonardo, *Liber Abaci* (Book of the Abacus, 1202); *Practica Geometriae* (Practice of Geometry, 1200); *Flos* (Prime Numbers, 1225); and *Liber Quadratorium* (Book of Squares. 1225). Only one letter has been found, one addressed from Leonardo to Magister Theodoris, philosopher to Emperor Frederick II.

As a youngster, Fibonacci was educated in the North African mathematics of Boufie (now Bejaia), Algeria, about 10 miles east of Algiers. His father was a warehouse manager and encouraged his son to receive a business education." Studying under a Moorish schoolmaster, Fibonacci soon learned to calculate using Arabic and Hindu figures – 0 through 9 – different than the then-dominant Roman symbols I, V, X, L, C, D, and M representing one, five, ten, fifty, one hundred, five hundred, and one thousand. The Roman system did not use 0. The simple procedures of division and multiplication were almost impossible in a merchant's world of commerce, hence the use of the abacus. It was in this environment that *Liber Abaci* appeared, a fifteen-chapter book on the new-to-Europe Arabic symbols that became a boon to western merchants. The volume explained how to read and write the numbers, and how to add, subtract, multiply and divide with them. Fractions and square roots were explained. The final chapter treated the subjects of algebra and geometry.

Europe's need of the Arabic numerals was evident to Fibonacci as he traveled throughout the Mediterranean region. His writings brought him fame in the field of mathematics. Emperor Frederick II was especially impressed by *Liber Abaci* and traveled to Pisa to stage a mathematics tournament for the area's leading mathematicians including Fibonacci. Three questions created by Johannes of Palermo were sent in advance to each contestant.

1. Squares: a second degree problem. Determine values of X and Y, such that $X^2 + 5 = Y^2$, when $X^2 - 5 = Y^2$

2. Cubes: a third degree problem, involving cubes

3. Riddle: a first degree problem

Three men owned respectively, a half, a third and a sixth of an unknown quantity of money. Each man took an unspecified amount of money, leaving a remainder of none. Each man in turn returned a half of a third and a sixth of what he had first taken. The returned money was divided into equal thirds and redistributed to the men. This resulted in each man acquiring his fair share.

QUESTION: determine the quantity of money owned by each man.

It is reported Fibonacci gave correct answers to each question while his competitors withdrew, unable to solve the problems.

Now, returning to the rabbits (and the famous Fibonacci Sequence):

It was the contribution to mathematics that brought Fibonacci his fame, topping even his accomplishment of bringing Arabic and Hindu numerals to a Western Europe stumbling with the burden of the Roman numeral system.

A pair of rabbits is kept in an enclosure and begins producing offspring at the rate of one pair each month, beginning in the second month. Each new pair reproduces at the same rate after its second month. Assuming no mortality, how many rabbits will exist at the end of a year?"

ANSWER–THE FIBONACCI SEQUENCE:
1, 2, 3, 5, 8, 13, 21, 34, 55, 89, 144, 233...

Each number is the sum of the two preceding numbers. The last two numbers in the series will combine to create another. If you divide a Fibonacci number by the next highest number, you will produce .618034 (reached after the 14th number in the sequence).

Thus the magic number: .618034

It is the .6 to 1 approximation which appears most appealing, in matters of perspective and proportion, in the size of playing cards and writing pads as examples, as well as in windows and a host of ordinary rectangular objects.

The Greeks did not achieve their sense of appropriate proportions by the use of .618034. They employed their own Golden Mean or Golden Proportion – that is – the "balance" achieved on a straight line by placing a mark which divides the line so that the lesser part is to the greater part as the greater part is to the total line. Johannas Kepler described the achievement of dividing a line into the extreme and mean ratio as a "precious jewel."

Author William Hoffer surmised that early recognition and evidence of the Golden Mean may "still be visible today on the plateau of Giza in Egypt." Egyptians may have based their work on a looser proportion of 5 to 8, the two early numbers of the Fibonacci Sequence that approximate the

Golden Mean but are slightly off. The average ratio of altitude to base of all Giza pyramids is roughly .625 or 5 to 8.

It is a magnificent step and a surge of brilliant adaptive logic to move from Golden Proportion to straight line, a step Jay Hambridge of Yale University describes as "static symmetry." By "smoothing out" the straight lines in whirling squares, a golden spiral is created. Jacob Bernoulli demonstrated the concept in the 17th century which Hoffer describes as the connection of center points of successive (whirling) squares which create "a sort of stiff spiral that works its way ever larger. Any section of the spiral is .618034 as large as the remainder of the spiral." Hence, the straight lines, curved outward, created a Golden Spiral.

Named the "logarithmic spiral" and also known as the "equiangular spiral," Bernoulli thought so highly of this achievement in mathematical insight that he gave orders for it to be engraved on his tombstone.

Readers wishing to delve more fully into the world of Golden Ratio and Fibonacci numbers (a world of mathematics especially impacting physics, geology, and computer technology), may want to consider *The Golden Ratio and Fibonacci Numbers* by Richard A. Dunlap as a most helpful and substantive resource. Dunlap thoughtfully cautions that formal mathematics has been kept to a minimum, although readers should have a general knowledge of algebra, geometry and trigonometry at the high school or first year university level.

It is in the realm of logarithmic spirals that we see the "golden mean" applied in nature, to the snail, the chambered nautilus; to sunflowers, pine cones, pineapples, plant stalks, leaf arrangement (phyllotaxis), animal teeth, claws, and horns; and the galaxies of outer space. In music, the E note vibration is .62500 to the C note – very close to the golden mean.

William Hoffer points out that a major ratio recurs "throughout all nature." Naturalist Sir D'Arcy W. Thompson similarly recounted that the shell and its tenant "grows in size but does not change its shape; and the existence of this constant relativity of growth, or constant similarity of form, is of the essence."

Hoffer concludes with the observation that the golden spiral is "nature's way of building quantity without sacrificing quality."

9

Survival ~ Extinction

*Society undergoes continual changes; it is barbarous, it is
civilized, it is Christianized, it is rich, it is scientific; but
this change is not amelioration, For everything that is
given something is taken."*
— *Ralph Waldo Emerson*

An article in the Los Angeles Times reported by
environmentalist Joshua Reichert, carried the headline
"One by One, the World is Becoming a Lonelier
Place." Worldwide, the extinction rate of species is increasing
at an alarming rate. The article might also have been
headlined, "Mariana mallard, Guam broadbill: R.I.P."

Starting with the announcement by the U.S. Fish and
Wildlife Service that two tropical birds, the Mariana mallard
and the Guam broadbill have disappeared from the face of
the earth, Reichert reflected upon these two seemingly
minuscule losses which testify to the larger regrettable
picture: currently some 12,000 plant and animal species are in
the "threatened" for extinction category. 1816 of these live in
the United States.

Why are these creatures and plants disappearing? Reichert cited human-induced pressures such as habitat loss, over-hunting, and the introduction of non-native species against which little or no defense mechanisms exist.

Why is the disappearance of two types of birds damaging? Each species plays a role and if even one disappears, it is a harbinger of trouble. We may conclude that the loss of two species, however remote, makes the world a little lonelier."

These thoughts helped me recall John Steinbeck's *Cannery Row* and the gopher who decided to take up residence in a vacant Cannery Row lot. It was a perfect spot, one with an abundance of green plants and soft dark earth with a good mixture of clay. He started his burrow on a slight hill which provided great drainage. The gopher was in the prime of his life and created a necessary passage way and storage rooms. He was especially pleased to find two great rocks, ideal for serving as the roofing for his main food chamber. All in all, it was a perfect place for settling down with a family and friends.

He cut large stems from the mallow plants into exact lengths and stored them in a way to prevent spoilage. He had found the perfect place for a home! He created side chambers for future baby gophers. Then he sat at the burrow entrance and made the usual chirping mating noises. No one came; no female appeared. Finally, he went out and explored another nearby lot and observed a community of gophers and their burrows.

Depressed and sad, he went back to his empty lot. There, no other gophers were found, no community. Finally, he realized he was forced to move to the already occupied lot, admittedly dangerous because of traps put out nightly.

I have long marveled at Steinbeck's understanding of the gopher's plight. It touches several great truths about the survival process, loneliness, and about taking necessary steps despite danger.

Years ago, in the town of El Monte, I had a neighbor who was afflicted with a gopher problem. The little animals almost destroyed his garden and gardening efforts regarding rhubarb plants (neighbor Irv loved rhubarb pie).

My interest in his problem started with the rhubarb because the plant was well known along the Volga River (longest in Europe) at a time when the river was named Rha and the plant was similarly named and finally translated into rhu-barb. My interest changed when I saw Irv setting traps, sprinkling poison pills, and dowsing the burrows with water – all to no avail.

The beautiful rhubarb stalks would disappear down the holes created by the determined gophers; nothing slowed them down. I really got interested when another neighbor joined the fray, a neighbor who was assertive and very convincing.

"The gophers were here a long time before you were," he told Irv. "They think the land is theirs and you're trying to drive them out. Put a candle on a little plate and write a note to the gophers. Tell them you're sorry for the trouble and that they can have half of the garden plot if you can have the front half. Tell them you'll keep their half planted in rhubarb. Light the candle, put the note where they can read it and go to bed. Your worries are over!"

Irv said he was never bothered by the gophers again.

I recall author Reichert's comment about human induced pressures, especially about the introduction of non-native species. I have watched groups of volunteers working hard, long hours, clearing a canyon of invasive, non-native plants so the indigenous growth might recoup and flourish.

It probably never occurred to members of the group that invasive, non-native Europeans wiped out the magnificent indigenous cultures of the Aztecs, Mayans, and Incas in our Western Hemisphere. Aggressive invasion has been a key to our culture's dominance. In this context, the sad goodbye to the Mariana mallard and the Guam broadbill (memorialized by the acronym R.I.P.) does not mean "Repeat Invasive Process."

10

Mythunderstanding

Error of opinion may be tolerated where reason is left free
to combat it."
  — Thomas Jefferson

Seldom has there been a more powerful, persuasive, brilliantly-presented published work than Rachel Carson's *Silent Spring*, presented to the American public in 1962 to enthusiastic acclaim. It was virtually adopted by concerned environmentalists.

Carson's appeal to all who love nature and nature's creatures, large and small, cannot be denied, nor should it be denied. We all yearn for freedom from disease and security from plagues. We want abundant wildlife living space; rivers, lakes, stream beds and the embracing seas and oceans to be free from pollution. We want the skies to be free from deleterious effluents.

That's why those of us who read *Silent Spring* cherished it almost from the very moment we saw Carson's dedicatory presentation to Albert Schweitzer, who said "Man has lost the capacity to foresee and forestall. He will end by destroying the earth."

That is why the first chapter of *Silent Spring: a Fable for Tomorrow* captivated us. A town in the heart of America filled with boundless grain fields, orchards, and healthy shade trees surrounded by green forests protecting foxes and deer! A strange blight followed – a shadow of death. Animals sickened and died: people – adults and children – died. There was a strange stillness that killed birds and withered the orchards. It was not witchcraft or the work of enemies that caused it, but the actions of the people themselves.

Carson pointed out that the town in her work does not exist, and she led with a dedicatory quote from Schweitzer. Dr. J. Gordon Edwards, a professor of entomology at San Jose State University asks in the publication *21ˢᵗ Century Science and Technology*, "Why did she not quote the relevant passage from Schweitzer's autobiography?" which asks "How much labor and waste of time these wicked insects do cause us … but a ray of hope, in the use of DDT, is now held out to us!"

A thoughtful person understands. Carson's first quotation from Schweitzer served her purpose, despite the fact that first quotation probably had to do with his concern about nuclear warfare. I believe, factually, Carson dedicated her work in error.

However, let's extend our understanding: her introductory chapter is described as, and admitted to be, myth. I was raised in an agricultural area, in a very small community. I never saw the terrors of a "Silent Spring." Our orchard filled with apples, pears, cherries, figs, and plums was healthy and abundant. Our animals were healthy and the foxes and birds thrived. We swam in the streams of the Chesapeake Bay in Virginia and our well water was potable. We used various protective chemical products very carefully, as required.

I have lived and worked in towns in California, Virginia, Washington D.C., and Texas. The few deserted and silent towns I have seen were the result of worked-out enterprises in lumber and mining. Where are the thousand counterparts of towns in America that suffered the "Silent Spring?"

To really understand Carson's position, one must consider the most overlooked and ignored paragraph in Carson's *Silent Spring*" in which she allows a need for insect control that must be "geared to realities" and not endanger humanity as well as the intended.

The observation is the most important of Rachael Carson's work, and is right, truthful, and complete. What a crime that many environmentalists, scientists, governmental bureaucrats and news media reporters have not realized the profound importance of Rachael Carson's conclusive concern!

A statement of such simplicity, integrity and practicality should be elevated to a similitude of "ten commandments" status and import. (On second thought, that would be self-defeating: included in such majestic status, it would then be forbidden to be displayed in public places for constitutional concerns in separation of Church and State!)

We humans share the water planet with one another, as well as the deer, foxes, cattle, birds, fish – all animals and insects. Indeed, one dominant religious group believes, because of ancient scriptures, that the Creator has allowed man to have "dominion" over the fish and fowl, the cattle, and all the earth, and over every "creeping thing that creepeth" the earth."

Carson's conclusion is a virtual "golden rule." It is worthy of respectful consideration. Vector control organizations in the U.S. and throughout the world, should make that Golden Rule the focus of their mission, the cynosure of all eyes watching vector control programs and progress.

In this connection, Carson's "geared to realities" reference is especially meaningful. The data commentary that follows will assist in comprehending the magnitude of the worldwide task.

Today, more than 2 billion people, some 40% of the world's population, live in malarial countries. 270 million are infected, and it is estimated that there are now more than 100 million clinical cases each year, some 300,000 new cases per day. Africa is the hardest hit, with nearly 35% of the world's cases. More than 30% of childhood deaths are directly caused by malaria, according to J. Gordon Edwards, who deplores what he considers to have been an irrational campaign of fear against pesticides which he attributes to Rachael Carson and her book.

Too few of us know about the horror of epidemics in U.S. port cities between 1668 and 1893. In 1793, yellow fever claimed one in ten Philadelphians, totaling some 4000 deaths. New Orleans is a frequent victim of attack and suffered 29,000 cases and over 8,000 deaths in 1853. During the summer of 1878, an epidemic swept the U.S. affecting 132 towns with 95,000 reported cases.

We do know – at least, most of us – that yellow fever and malaria defeated the French attempt to build a canal across the Isthmus of Panama, killing a third of the work force every year from 1881 to 1889.

The Panama Convention was signed in 1903. William C. Gorgas, who had served as sanitary officer in Cuba and discovered that yellow fever was spread by mosquitoes (aedes aegypti), then moved on to Panama. Gorgas believed malaria was a bigger problem. The central strategies for this disease differ somewhat and relied primarily on converting swamps to dry land. When it could not be accomplished, anopheles larvae were killed by oiling the water surface.

A most direct, practical op-ed commentary published in the *New York Times* by Dr. Henry I. Miller of Stanford University describes the increasing possibility of a serious West Nile virus outbreak, noting that in 2003 there were over 4000 cases and some 300 deaths. The mosquito-borne virus has been found in 38 states.

Miller's observations stand as lighthouses sending flashes of alarm against potential disaster. He notes that lacking a vaccine, the elimination of the transmission organism of the West Nile virus – the mosquito – is the key to prevention. There exist fundamental shortcomings in public policy limiting the tools available."

In 1972, on the basis of dubious data about toxicity to fish and migrating birds, the Environmental Protection Agency banned virtually all uses of the pesticide DDT, an inexpensive and effective pesticide. DDT was once widely deployed to kill disease-carrying insects.

Given that other pesticides lack long-term effectiveness, DDT may be the best alternative to fighting mosquitoes and the West Nile virus. It's worth recalling that DDT aided in eradicating malaria from the United States.

Miller recommends draining what he terms the "public policy swamps," through government re-evaluation of data regarding DDT, in hopes of making it available for mosquito control in the United States. Additionally, he opposes international strictures on DDT that burden the developing countries, many of which are plagues by malaria.

He suggests that federal officials should campaign to educate local authorities and citizens about the safety and importance of DDT.

My responsibilities on the Greater Los Angeles County Vector Control District Board of Trustees require me to make every effort to protect the public from the serious impacts of disease. In 2004, West Nile virus presented such a challenge.

Fortunately, we have one of the most skilled, experienced, and dedicated staffs in the U.S., a group prepared to exert every effort to meet the anticipated West Nile virus mosquito-borne challenge.

Our district has in place a $500,000 emergency reserve fund to prepare for and respond to West Nile virus. Some of these funds have been spent to obtain and stockpile additional mosquito pesticides. Other funds cover expenditures for recently-hired personnel to augment the district's underground storm drainage program. Source surveillance efforts continue; a five-mile radius centered in the epicenter of the 2003 activity will be surveyed by air. Sentinel chicken flocks have been increased and adult mosquito traps will be added. Hospital and HMO resource cooperation will be sought for submitting human blood samples. Abatement notices will be issued to both public and private property owners whose holdings reflect a public nuisance as defined by state health and safety codes.

Additionally, an outreach program directed at some 900,000 homeowners urges the ridding of backyard standing water and related breeding areas.

Our vector control district is prepared. It will get the job done, professionally and safely.

The problems and outcomes of other countries are of considerable concern. India, China, Pakistan, and third-world countries all face huge plague and disease challenges, especially in funding responses, acquiring public support and technical resources. How will they cope if West Nile virus appears? Globalization brings nations closer. Nascent far-away problems may become next-door anxieties. Disease moves swiftly and strikes indiscriminately.

In Steven J. Milloy's 2001 work *Junk Science Judo; Self-defense against Health Scares and Scams*, he notes that millions die and hundreds of millions suffer from malaria. He then notes that the banning of DDT flies in the face of expert testimony that promotes DDT as effective in reducing deaths and suffering.

Manoo Madon is the scientific and technical services director of the greater Los Angeles County vector district. He says the effects of malaria can be offset by worldwide use of DDT to dramatically reduce the number of human cases as well as fatalities. Malaria is just one example of mosquito-borne diseases. Untold numbers of louse-borne cases were prevented by the use of DDT. Several other diseases transmitted by insects and food-destroying agricultural pests can be reduces by DDT usage.

Regardless of whether a product is good or bad, human nature is such that we tend to go astray when it comes to its usage. As a result, it is arguable that some damage may have been caused by its indiscriminate and irresponsible use.

However, we must take into consideration the benefits versus the claimed damages DDT may have caused. Millions of human lives were saved and millions more cases of illness were prevented. The savings amount to trillions of dollars.

I cannot help but think of Cervantes' carefully chosen symbol, Don Quixote de la Mancha. The knight-errant on his weary steed Rozinante, was accompanied by the "shallow brained" Sancho Panza in preparing to meet life's problems. He had "grievances to address, wrongs to rectify, errors to amend, abuses to reform, debts to discharge."

What a mission!

Equipped with his great-grandfather's rusty armor and an incomplete helmet outfitted with a visor of paste board, Don Quixote rode to contest what dreadful giant, which windmill?

How will a poor country fare, facing plague and disease – or an unexpected giant such as the West Nile virus?

11

The Magic of Peru

Animater of the Universe ~ creator of human beings.
Lords of Lords, I wish to look at you with my imperfect
eyes.
    —Inca prayer to Wiracocha translated by Joan
Pachacuti

Before Columbus "discovered" America, the people who inhabited Peru, the Children of the Sun, created a great Quechua-Inca Empire extending along South America's west coast. Unlike the Mayan and Aztec cultures, the Inca Empire embraced one of the major desert coastal areas in the world as well as thousand of miles of the great Andes range that dominates South America.

Today's Peru – a republic – is the third largest country in South America with a population of some twenty-seven million. It is a nation drained and exhausted after a decade of internecine warfare by the *Sendero Luminsos*. Peru is finally enjoying the luxury of relative tranquility. The August 29, 2003 report of the National Truth and Reconciliation Committee" documents the end of the nightmare and horror of some 69,000 deaths and disappearances.

Peru is enjoying the resumption of Quechua Aztec inheritances and the Hispanic-Anglo dominance of Lima and the capitol city's modernity. Tourism flourishes. The major attractions for visitors remain the Inca-based communities in the Sacred Valley including Cusco, the center of the Quechua - Inca; monumental Machu Picchu; Huacachina lagoon, an oasis in the midst of giant dunes.

Visitors to this wonderful country soon learn the basics of Incan Culture. The Cusco (which translates as navel) region was the hub of the far-flung, four-sector governmental imperium. Inti was the sun god and thunder, lightning, and rainbows were considered Inti's manifestations. Cuzco, the city that was the capital of the Cusco region, was founded much like Tenochtitlan, today's Mexico City. The Sun God's two children, placed on an island in Lake Titicaca, were given a golden staff and told to search the land and find the spot where the staff, when plunged into the earth, would instantly disappear. That spot became the Inca's capitol city – Cusco – at an elevation of 11,300 feet.

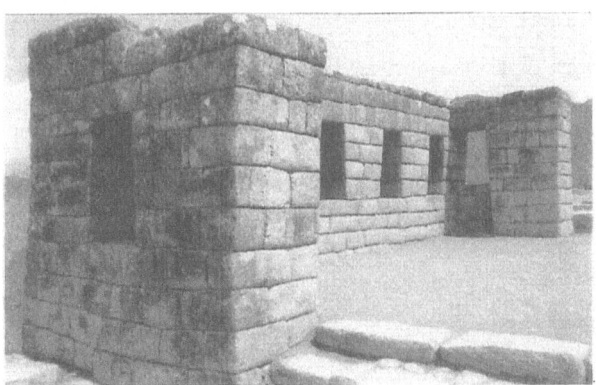

Ancient Incan Stone Construction in Peru

The Incas were master stone builders, unsurpassed tapestry weavers, skillful surgeons, and competent craftsmen in the working of bronze, copper, silver and gold.

Their social system included three classes; imperial, nobility, and common people. Family households were grouped into units of ten and major subdivisions would include some 40,000 households. The economic system has been described as one providing the masses of people with far more than any modern society today. Immense land areas were divided into three portions: one for the Sun (support of state religion); one for the Inca (government); one for the tribal (family) group. Of note is the strict labor code exempted from farm labor and farm tribute: Inca caste, nobility, sun priests, soldiers, males under 25 and over 50, all women, the sick, and the blind. The lame and maimed were exempted. Basic to governmental policy were a common language, over-all colonization system, abundance for all, an imperium roadway system, and an effective communication medium (quipu-based).

Of the five areas basic to governmental policy, Incan communication presents the greatest puzzle for archeologists, mathematicians, and researchers: what was the Inca medium employed to achieve effective communication? What is meant by "quipu-based?"

There are no known inscribed Inca writings on parchment, wood, clay, or stone. The vast, sophisticated, and powerful Inca Empire existed without the amenity of writing, unlike other major cultures (Mayan, Aztec). There has been no Inca-language discovery such as Egypt's Rosetta Stone.

The quipu – or khipu – (as opposed to Quechua, a language still prevalent in the Andes), involves multi-layered knotted cotton strings hanging from a large fiber. A quipu would circle the waist of an Inca message-runner who covered many miles to deliver the messages knotted on the often colored strings.

Currently, Harvard researchers are studying quipus found at an archeological site called Purochuco, some 5 miles east of Peru's capitol of Lima. Quipus are sacred. Spanish freebooting invaders believed them to be symbols of idols and destroyed them by the thousands, forcing the Incan adoption of the European system of writing. It is estimated there exists some 700 quipus worldwide in museums and research centers. The oldest, discovered in 2004 by Peruvian archaeologist Ruth Shady, is thought to be at least 4000 years old. It was discovered in the pre-Inca city of Caral, one of the largest cities in western hemisphere history.

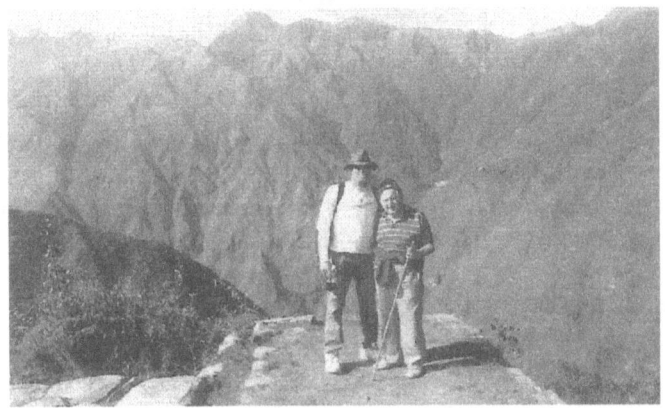

Author and Son in Peru

Some researchers believe the quipu system involved knotted strings representing a numeric, decimal-based shorthand. Others speculate that a hierarchical accounting system was involved. Some see a yet-unsolved written language – perhaps phonetic Quechua shorthand. Some report a belief that a first step in solving the puzzle has been taken in the identification in the knotted strings of the name of the city where the quipos were found – the city of Purochuco.

Juan Larrea wrote in *Machu Picchu: City of Eternal Hope*, that travelers are taken by a "rare and unfamiliar euphoria" upon visiting that ancient place. Presumably constructed in the 1400's, the lost city of the Incas was never "lost," nor was it discovered by the invading Spanish marauders who sacked half of the Western hemisphere.

Parenthetically, I now understand Gandhi's devastating response to the question: "What do you think of Western civilization?" He is quoted as replying, "I think it would be a good idea."

Manchu Picchu formed a religious retreat and astronomical observatory for some 700 religious and astrophysical-oriented persons. When word came that the Spanish invaders were attacking the Inca capitol, Cuzco, the Machu Picchu workers and guards left to defend the central city. Alone on the mountain range, with their food supply route cut off and water system threatened for want of care, the community of Machu Picchu faced starvation and death. They abandoned their mountain retreat and moved downward and eastward into the vast Amazon Basin.

High jungle growth slowly covered the City. Not until 1911 was the "Lost City" re-discovered by the American explorer and archaeologist Hiram Bingham, a former professor at Yale University and U.S. Senator from Connecticut. He led an expedition into the Urubamba Valley and uncovered Machu Picchu.

Removing the forest growth and reclaiming the city followed. The National Geographic Society and its renowned magazine brought the discovery to a fascinated public.

Machu Picchu was constructed at the elevation of about 8000 feet on a long ridge that drops sharply some 1500 feet to the Urubamba River. There one sees the carefully preserved and beautiful plazas, temples, store buildings, homes, irrigation channels, and terraced slopes of an amazing rectilinear city with a central fixture, the Temple of the Sun. The west wall of the temple runs long and straight, and was described by Bingham as "the most beautiful wall in America."

Everything is overwhelming. The great pyramidal backdrop of Huayna Picchu with its snow clad peak highlights an encircling river that vanishes into the Amazon Basin. The interactive harmony, balance and beauty of this City of the Sky, a city of science, religion, and sophistication, is one in which the stones still speak and the enfolding environment sings.

For me (and for my son Dexter and his wife, who made possible the birthday-gift trip), it was the experience of a lifetime. For two days we walked a portion of the Inca trail above Machu Picchu. Dexter and Nancy, both world-class athletes, had no trouble with the narrow, twisting trail-way. I struggled with the altitude and with the steep, rugged pathways ascending and descending seemingly interminable slopes.

As an 86-year-old, I wasn't fit to cope. When we arrived at our viewpoint destination, the guides at the lodge said that – in their collective memories – I was the oldest person to have made that portion of the hike. The reward made it worthwhile. We walked the city's stone ways, marveled at the irrigation canals, rested and meditated on the plazas. Words scarcely explain. Simply, it was Manchu Picchu Magic!

The 8th of June 1998 marked the death of 93-year-old Dr. Maria Reiche-Grosse. Born in 1905 at Dresden, Germany she was a graduate of programs in mathematics, geography, and astronomy. She arrived in Peru in 1932 and taught science in Cusco. She first investigated the astronomical calendar at Manchu Picchu called the Intihuatana Stone, sometimes called the place to which the sun is tied.

In 1941 Maria began her studies of the "Lines" between Palpa and Nazca. She became known worldwide as the Lady of the Lines. The Peruvian Government gave her the official title of Honorary Keeper of the Archaeological Site, and on December 17, 1994, UNESCO officials declared the Lines and figures of Palpa as a "world culture heritage."

Maria considered the "mysterious ground drawings in the region of the tributaries of the Rio Grande, provinces of Nazca and Palpa, as documentation of an ancient calendar-science of the Nazca culture and a creation described by historian Dr. Paul Kosok of Long Island University as "the longest astronomy book in the world." Dr. Kosok is credited with the discovery of the mysterious ground drawings in the Peruvian department of Ica. He turned his findings over to Maria Reiche.

In *The Mystery of the Desert* she emphasizes that the art and the colossal and mysterious stone structures are evidence of a once highly-developed civilization. The dynasty of the Incas represents, only the last stage of a long cultural evolution, one with beginnings reaching back to the second millennium BC

There are many theories about the origins, meaning, and significance of the mysterious Nazca Lines and the multitude of figures located principally in the vast desert flatlands between the towns of Palpa and Nazca, west of the Andes Mountains and some 400 km south of Lima. The Pan American Sur Highway runs through the Lines.

It is noteworthy that the Lines were called Inca trails by the local inhabitants. Archaeological studies were published in 1926 but it was not until 1941 that Professor Kosok realized the lines might have solstice-related relevance.

Several major theories have been advanced in an attempt to solve the mystery of the Lines, including one proposing they represent the world's largest astronomical calendar, developed and constructed by the Nazca between 100 AD and 600 AD.   Another purports them to be images of magic origin presumed to have been venerated as religious symbols and pathways for pilgrimages. Other theories lay responsibility for the presence of the Lines to extraterrestrials who built them as landing strips.

This concept embraces the notion that long-ago astronauts from a far-away world created the Lines before returning to their home planet, a contention supported by the presence of dozens of gigantic figures such as birds, fish, monkeys, hands, dogs, spiders, fans, flowers, and trees. Among the more controversial figures is the Astronaut, also called the Owl Head Man.

Why were the Lines and giant figures not discovered and researched long ago? What kept them apart until 1939?

The huge dimensions of these lines and figures are barely discernable from ground level, making them almost impossible to see. It took airplanes to help man identify the lines and when viewed from high above, the Lines were first thought to be irrigation canals. When Dr. Kosok first visited the area to study irrigation practices, he thought he was looking down on extensive waterways. When he later examined the lines at ground level it amounted to the discovery – more accurately, the understanding – of the "Lines." He handed his information to Maria Reiche, who accepted the task and started her many-years-long labor to measure, categorize, and preserve the unbelievably mysterious and centuries-old historical treasure.

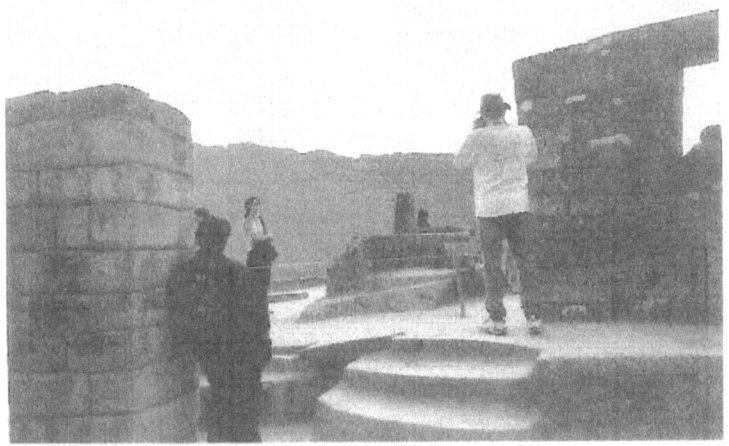

Intihuatana Stone: Solar Observatory Arc

It is now understood, just as the Great Pyramids of Egypt are easily seen because of their three-dimensional construction at ground level, that the Lines and figures of Peru are almost impossible to see at ground level. They require a higher visual perspective.

Many of the Lines extend for a mile and the figures are expansive as well; the spider is 150' long; long-necked bird is over 380' long; and the crocodile over 600'long. Twenty of the figures represent birds.

So exactly parallel are thousand-foot-long double lines, so perfect are proportions of spirals, so exact are curves and dimensions, so great the size – how could all that be achieved to such a successful extent that current aerial photographs prove them to be perfect?

Maria Reiche surmised that that the ancient Peruvians must have had instruments and equipment unknown to us, and those – along with their ancient knowledge were buried and hidden from the eyes of the conquerors.

12

Appraising: Business or Profession?

A bill of rights is what the people are entitled to against every government on earth."
—*Thomas Jefferson*

There are perhaps some 200,000 appraisal practitioners in the United States. Of this number, it is estimated that approximately 40,000 are members of one of the five major nationwide testing and certifying appraisal societies. The majority of practitioners are concerned with the discipline of real property valuations.

Why should anyone be interested in appraising? If you own real property in the United States, for example – your home – it is probably taxed annually. How does the tax assessor know how much the property is worth? Someone representing the taxing agency appraised your property.

This commentary introduces you to that "someone" and the process. In addition to taxation, when buying, selling, or getting a loan on a home, the appraisal becomes a significant item.

Again – meet your appraiser.

Appraisers are unique because their business specialty and expertise include a responsibility inherited from cultural concepts formed perhaps 2,500 years ago, concepts that have challenged rulers and governments and have been at the heart of revolutions.

It is the purpose of this commentary to trace the historic thread of cultural concepts and identify the revolutionary impacts; to present a summary of the emergence of appraising in the United States. (One major appraisal society will be utilized to illustrate growth, programs, and challenges in the world of appraising; and to analyze factors which challenge present-day appraisal societies.

John Adams noted that personal rights preceded governments, "rights that cannot be repealed or restricted by human laws." Those rights, he claimed, were "derived from the great Legislator of the Universe."

Adam's description deals with the higher law and would have found immediate acceptance in ancient Greece and Rome. It was a concept introduced into Greco-Roman jurisprudence and was welcomed as an explanation of *jus gentium* to be championed by jurists including Gaius, Ulpain and Cicero. It was well documented that the inherent power of government to appropriate private property for a public use was exercised in many ways. Affirmation of the "Higher Law" in the writings of Plato, Aristotle, Aeschylus, Sophocles, and Euripides emphasizes the theory of "Higher Law" stands in direct contrast to the positive theory of law as the "Command of a Sovereign."

It was in England that the confrontation of the Higher Law was most severely challenged by the concept and enforcement of the King's Prerogative. Blackstone commented during his lectures at Oxford that "the limit of the King's prerogative was deemed a topic too sacred to be prepared by the pen of a subject."

It was the cumulative effect of abuses of the sovereign power that forced John, King of England, to meet the English Barons who gathered in the meadow which is called

Runnymede between Windsor and Staines on June 15, 1215. The concessions there seized and recorded affected the mainstream of English life, the common law and, ultimately, the colonies – including America. The Great Charter, written in Latin (the barons spoke French) has been divided into 63 chapters by scholars. Chapter 39 contains the supreme contribution which Magna Carta preserved for the World, and declares that "No free man shall be taken, dissseised, outlawed, banished or in any way destroyed, nor will we proceed against or prosecute him, except by the lawful judgment of his peers and by the law of the land."

The key word is *disseised*, which – in law – is to deprive of *seisen*, or of the possession of a freehold interest in land.

It was about four centuries later that a Dutch jurist named Huig de Groot, also known as Hugo Grotius, first and formally articulated the scope, extent and effective of the power which he called *Eminens Dominius* and conjoined the concept with the obligation to make good the loss. (*De Juri Belli, ac Oacis* – 1625)

Similarly, Otto Gierke's 19th century declaration in *Political Theories of the Middle Ages* surmises that "when there is expropriation for the good of the public, compensation should be made at public expense."

William Blackstone, in 1765, published *Commentaries on the Law* and asserted that "In this and similar cases, the legislature alone can interpose and compel the individual to acquiesce." It was his contention that all that the legislature does is to oblige the owner to "alienate his possessions for a reasonable price."

England's several colonies in America, inheritors of the Common Law of England, enacted a Declaration of Independence in 1776, a document which did not speak of property rights in the sense of confrontation between sovereign and citizen.

The Constitution contains provisions regarding public taking of private property for compensation. It is article five of the Bill of Rights that contains these particular safeguards.

Article 5 contains about 110 words. The last 12 emerge from our research through some 2,500 years as: "nor shall private property be taken from public use, without just compensation."

For those who are aware that *The Federalist*, a powerful series of articles written by Hamilton, Madison and Jay as a commentary on the Constitution, does not advocate adoption of a Bill of Rights. It is nonetheless a shock to read in that work that "bill of rights are not only unnecessary in the proposed Constitution, but would even be dangerous."

It is amazing. During the same year (1791) that our Bill of Rights was accepted as an amendment to the Constitution, a similar expression of the individual's rights was affirmed in France. "The Declaration of the Rights of Man and Citizen" (a most famous document connected with the French Revolution) was incorporated into the French Constitution of 1791.

Article 17 provides that property, "being a sacred and invisible right," of ownership and that "no one can be deprived of it unless a legally established public necessity demands it, under the condition of a just and prior indemnity."

It must be remembered that America was an emergent nation and that France was endowed with a national history exceeding 1000 years. Both addressed property rights issues in their new organic institutional documents.

Additionally, France formally adopted in 1804 the Napoleonic Code composed of three major books: *Of Persons*; *Of Property*; and *Modes of Acquiring Property*. This magnificent code dominates the civil law world, including Belgium, Mauritus, Scotland, South Africa, Spain, Central America, South America, Cuba, Mexico, The Philippines, Province of Quebec, portions of the West Indies, and Louisiana. Additionally, the Code impacted legal concepts in Japan, China, Turkey, Egypt, Lebanon, and Syria.

Our world of the common law includes the U.S. except Louisiana; Canada, except the Province of Quebec; and Great Britain.

I am persuaded the intense scrutiny given property, property rights and just compensation throughout centuries of struggle, confrontation and rebellion, has conveyed a message that convinces most of those who enter the appraisal world to become engaged in the real estate discipline of appraisal.

This country's appraisal practitioners emerged in the 1920's and early 1930's, and early efforts were directed toward the identification of organizational structures and the establishing of educational and ethical criteria. It was during this time that the construction of discipline parameters occurred, seeking public recognition for the emergent profession.

An 1895 grain elevator fire in St. Paul, Minnesota, involved the services of court reporter John Morn and building contractor William Young. Their experience led them to form an insurance appraisal organization in Chicago. On February 1, 1896, American Appraisal Company was born. Also in 1896, the Coats and Burchard Company was created in Chicago, and General Appraisal Company was incorporated on 1902. Lloyd-Thomas Company was formed in 1910, headquartered in Chicago. There followed Industrial Appraisal Company; Manufacturers Appraisal company, and Marshall - Stevens Appraisal Company. In 1929, the American Society of Farm Managers and Rural Appraisers was formed in Denver, Colorado.

Passage in 1913 of the Sixteenth Amendment authorized Congress to "lay and collect taxes on incomes." Taxes could be reduced by claiming fixed assets depreciation but documentation to sustain claims was required, including appraisal reports achieved by objective third parties.

The formative years of appraisal practice produced little literature revealing pedestrian events. Fortunately, a major exception to this paucity is the self-published recollections of

Earl Pack Marshall, a California valuation expert. *Fifty Years of Change* was released on the occasion of his 88th birthday. His story covers the years 1927 - 1977.

Marshall's California appraisal assignments included his assignment to a Culver City movie studio to set values on the standing sets of the just-completed film *King of Kings*. With a clipboard in hand, he strolled down the fictional New York and Chicago streets setting "dollar values on the imaginative creations of the movie industry."

The small buildings housing the principal dressing rooms on the lot were occupied by Gloria Swanson and Eric Von Stroheim.

Marshall faced additional valuation puzzles at Republic Studio in Studio City, where he had to appraise a water tank "built for filming swimming antics."

In 1932, the Marshall Valuation Service was formed. Also in 1932, the National Association of Real Estate Boards created the American Institute of Real Estate Appraisers. 1935 saw a group of savings and loan appraisers form the Society of Real Estate Appraisers.

In his memoir, Marshall describes the formation, by the American Society of Technical Appraisers (of California) and the Technical Valuation Society of Appraisers (New York), of the American Society of Appraisers. The group initially had 18 chapters nationally, but expanded rapidly across the U.S. and Canada. In Washington D.C., an international headquarters was set up to coordinate and regulate their rapid progress.

As a former founding father, I have proudly watched the growth and development of the ASA.

I've chosen the American Society of Appraisers (ASA) as an illustration since the ASA is unique as the only major appraisal society with a decades-long record of representing all classes of property.

The ASA, in their *Principles of Appraisal Practice and Code of Ethics,* support institutions of higher learning in programs designed to provide the necessary academic background to both "appraisal aspirants" and those "who desire to upgrade and broaden their appraisal skills."

My personal practice as a member of the Virginia Bar included experience in eminent domain and condemnation proceedings, years-long experience in right of way appraisals within the state of California, and 13 years as executive vice-president of ASA in Washington D.C. This background gives me unique and substantive insight into the appraisal world and ASA.

1952 saw the introduction in the U.S. world of appraising of the concept of multiple-disciplines in valuation. This was achieved by the formation of ASA and its affirmation of the multi-discipline concept in its *Code of Ethics* and *Principles of Appraisal Practice.*

Cooperative participation with other appraisal societies began in 1960, accomplished by participating in the creation of the North American Conference of Appraisal Organizations, composed of the ASA, Appraisal Institute of Canada, American Society of Farm Managers and Rural Appraisers, and the Society of Real Estate Appraisers.

Support in 1968 provided the introduction of a professional, academically-oriented appraisal textbook into the academic and appraisal worlds. This was achieved by the production of Dr. Henry Babcock's seminal and scholarly work, *Appraisal Principles and Procedures."*

The significance of the legal pronouncements or court adjudications in 1969 regarding topics such as just compensation, indemnification, recompense, and "make good the loss," brought legal focus on market value and its definition.

Market value is the highest price estimated in terms of money which land would bring if sold in the open market, providing reasonable time in which to find a knowledgeable purchaser. This challenge was achieved with ASA's publication of the monograph *Power and Progress,* an examination of California's leading case: Sacramento Southern Railroad Company vs. Heilborn, 156 Cal. 406.

In 1973, a medium to confront valuation problems and issues was presented to the appraisal world, a medium similar to a Supreme Court, with authorization to issue opinions. Those judgments could facilitate understanding and eventual settlement of major valuation issues. This major challenge was accomplished when the ASA College of Fellows was formally organized in 1973 and authorized to prepare and publish *Opinions to Assist the Profession*.

From 1970 to 1978, there was a strengthening of the non-real estate appraisal disciplines. Two programs were to initiate the challenge, including the publication of a series of member-produced monographs directed to the minor disciplines. Those included "Insurance Valuations," "Icons of the Community," "Personal Property Appraisal," "Ad Valorem Appraising," "The New Professionals," and "The Appraisal of Machinery and Equipment." Secondly, the ASA created and published *The Bibliography of Appraisal Literature*. It was a first in the U.S. – a four-year project filling 769 pages and representing the specific areas of the multiple disciplines of appraising.

It is astonishing that the appraisal world had not produced such a bibliography long before. Indeed, it seems a blanket of silence exists about the early days and early achievement.

It resembles a similar unawareness of historical events: The renowned historian Thucydides wrote in his 5th century BC work, *History of the Peloponnesian War* that prior to the war, the evidence pointed to a conclusion that "before this time, nothing of significance" had happened.

The challenge from 1972 to 1976 was to create an audio-library, enabling ASA members to speak out on valuation-oriented topics. 65 "Valutapes" were produced, including the most controversial *Redlining and Appraisers* and *Opportunities in Appraising for Minorities*.

The Department of Justice in 1977 asked the ASA to assist in suggesting proper appraisal techniques regarding sensitive neighborhood factors in the appraisal of single family homes. Such topics as the "impact of homogeneity" on residential values were addressed. In response, the ASA prepared, presented, and taped a seminar on *Urban Disinvestment: Redlining and Residential Evaluation*, which was first presented at Hofstra University in Hempstead, NY, on April 30, 1997.

I was directly involved from 1972 to 1979 (on behalf of ASA) in efforts to remove restraints to professional appraisal practice, addressing laws, policies, procedural memoranda, and guidelines. In 157 instances, the work involved governmental agencies at federal, state, city, and county levels and private organizations representing a variety of business interests, including banks, savings and loans, and related financial institutions. Additionally, several of the major appraisal societies had representation. Of the 157 instances, seven did not prove amenable to a readjustment of their restrictive policy or procedure restraints in order to achieve equitable recognition of all professional competent-designated appraisal practitioners.

1973 through 1993 constituted the years of the Great Challenge, in the question of accomplishing education and the achieving and securing of professional status. How was it accomplished?

At a 1973 conference, it was stated that U.S. appraisers enter the profession by chance, and that "few initially planned their careers to be in appraising."

A timeline of accomplishments includes:

- January 1974: ASA adopts resolution re valuation science degree program concepts
- December 1974: Dr. Samuel Gould, former chancellor at New York State University agrees to serve as ASA Educational Consultant
- February 1975: ASA mails 4,486 VS degree program questionnaires to society members. Majority responds "strongly supportive."
- April 1975: ASA meets with representatives of the Incorporated Society of Valuers and Auctioneers

(ISVA) of London, England at the University of Reading's Centre for Advanced Land Use Studies, regarding Academic Appraisal Degree curricula.

- May 1975: ASA holds Valuation Sciences Degree Program meeting with some 20 educational institutes, including Virginia Polytechnic Institute; Eastern Carolina College; Florida State University; Washington International College; George Washington University; Park College; Drake University; Immaculate College, PA.; C.W. Post Center, NY; University of Hartford; Oakland University, Michigan; Skidmore College; Loretto Heights College; University of Minnesota UWW; University of Alabama UWW; Dyke College; University of Redlands-Johnston College; Pepperdine University; The Lindenwood Colleges' Evergreen State College.

- July, 1975: ASA meets with Atlanta University; Howard University; Southern University-New Orleans; Texas Southern University; Winston-Salem; Hampton Institute.

- December 1975: ASA forms National Education Advisory Council. Invitations to participate in the Valuation Sciences Degree Program issued to the Union of Experimental Colleges/Universities (consortium of 31); Northern Illinois University; Carolina; Positive Futures, Inc.

- June 1976: ASA Memorandum of Understanding reached with Hofstra University - New College, involving a Master of Arts Program and a University without Walls Undergraduate Program-BA Degree.

- October 1976: ASA College of Fellow issues an "Opinion" which includes the following: ". . .it is the consensus of this College that it is to the best interest of those who practice appraising that formal education programs be pursued within academic parameters; that a specific degree designed for the specialty of appraising will best achieve recognition for this emerging profession."

- February 1978: ASA's Valuation Sciences Degree Program brochures mailed to approximately 50,000 appraisers in the US, Canada, Puerto Rico, and the Philippines.

- April 1978: The Valuation Sciences Degree Program details are placed on the agenda of the North American Appraisal Conference organization (NACAO). At that meeting, Dr. Van Fossen, Sr., V.P. Association of Federal Appraisers, declared: "Bartlett, in his [work] *The Occupational Status of the Appraiser* states 'Before we can attain the status of a Profession, we must turn over to the Universities all of the fundamental appraisal education. We must take our heads out of the sand.'"

- May 1979: The first Valuation Sciences Masters Degree issued in the United States was presented by Hofstra University New College (Hempstead, New York). The historic thesis involved had a singularly appropriate title: "An Examination of Appraisal Practice in the United States: History, Current Structure, Major Issues, Movement for Trade Status to Professionalism."   Seventeen additional degrees were issued: topics included "Porcelain Appraisal"; "Business Valuation"; "Mass Appraisal"; "American Painting"; "Silver Judaica"; "Assessment Process"; "Antiquities"; "Machinery/Equipment"; and "Ceramics Valuation".

SPECIAL SECTION

U.S. Appraisal Practice: Challenges - the Legal Viewpoint

March 1976: (a) The most important and conclusive assault upon the comfortable and generally accepted assumption that "appraising is a profession" and that designated appraisers are considered professionals appears in a March 1976 legal decision (Rosenbloom vs. State Tax Commission) issued by the Supreme Court of New York. In the case (involving a real estate appraiser with 24 years of acknowledged appraisal experience and a designation from a major appraisal society), the court decided that the term 'professional' implies "knowledge gained by a prolonged course of specialized instruction and study." The Court further held that the petitioner "is not engaged in the practice of a profession."

March, 1976; (b) A second ruling, in which the Office of the Attorney General, State of California, concluded that state certified appraisers would not be considered professional employees. Upon juxtaposition of the knowledge, skills and education requirements of appraisers certified for appraisal tax purposes the office determined that such appraisers should not be considered "professional employees within the meaning of the Statute."

It has been several decades since I have been absorbed in the work and fortune of the world of appraising. I cherish the earned acronym FASA (Fellow, American Society of Appraisers) and I am as proud of my Hofstra University Master's Degree in Interdisciplinary Studies-Valuation Sciences as I am of long-ago honors of LLB and JD.

I remain impressed that the American Society of Appraisers nearly ascended as a group into the elite realm of the "Professions".

However, despite the enthusiasm initially generated and displayed in board meetings, educational conferences, chapter meetings, specialty seminars and the initial impressive successes at Hofstra University, it became apparent there were major impeditive reactions regarding the Valuation Sciences Degree Program.

Many appraisers stated they were "too pressured" by the intensity of their appraisal assignments. Taking time off and consequently losing assignments, then paying for college and university courses were factors considered too onerous and unacceptable. Additionally, many felt that short society-taught courses somehow "got the job done." Too, some of the appraisal societies were accustomed to making impressive incomes via their own "courses" and were reluctant to relinquish a good thing.

"Each one - teach one" worked fairly well. Of concern to many appraisers was the time it would take to get a degree in appraising."

There were other obstacles, including some raised by the college and university representatives themselves. Of concern was the lack of professors trained in the basic concepts and procedures of appraising. Institutions did not have the time, staff, or budgets to create the academic matrices involved. Several representatives were concerned that the number of appraisers constituted a small population and would prove to be too small a base to warrant special academic recognition.

The American Society of Appraisers shows little evidence of its former interest, pride and support of the Valuation Science Degree Program. I see few publications pursuing the concept of achieving professionalism via a relevant academic degree.

I hope some day, a new generation of appraisers will accept the challenge to climb the Mt. Everest of legally and academically recognized Professional Status. The economic and legal worlds deserve the attendance and competence of professionals.

13

The Bayeux ~ Tillett Tapestries

*Both tapestries are Art treasures. Scenes from the Bayeux
are displayed in the Victoria Albert Museum in London.
In Normandy, when the Tillett Tapestry went on display,
the crowds overwhelmed the cathedral.*
   –D. Dupont, in his Commentaries

Two of the world's greatest art treasures are the Bayuex
Tapestry depicting the Norman Conquest of England,
and the Tillett Tapestry of the Spanish Arrival in
Aztec Mexico. Each contains an exquisite depiction of
massive cultural impacts.

The Bayeux Tapestry is old – estimated to have been
created about 1092. One theory holds that Matilda, wife of
William the Conqueror, created the tapestry. Another
suggests it was commissioned by Odo, the bishop of Bayeux,
the conqueror's half-brother, and that it was produced in
England.

Whatever the date, the Bayeux tapestry has served as a
symbolic centerpiece to decorate the nave of Bayeux's gothic
cathedral. It survived the Great Revolution, highlighted
Napoleon's 1883 - 1904 Exhibition, and witnessed the World

War II occupation and recapture. It is of note that Bayeux was the first French town to be liberated from German occupation.

The town of Bayeux is located at the heart of Baie de la Seine, west of Le Havre and about 10 miles from Omaha Beach. It is perhaps 25 miles from Utah Beach, another name especially significant to the United States.

Suffice it to say, the Bayeux Tapestry (now light brown in color) is very old; a portion at the end has perished. It has been restored more than once and in some details the "restoration" is of doubtful authority.

Despite the wear and tear, it is agreed the 231-feet long and 20-inches wide band of linen, embroidered in worsteds (twisted yarn spun from combed long-staple wool) of light colors and depicting some 72 scenes, tells the story of the Norman conquest of England. The top and bottom of the cloth contain borders decorated with a variety of Aesop Fable scenes, agricultural views, and symbols related to the tapestry narrative.

It is recognized that this magnificent artwork has great pictorial significance. It mirrors medieval fables as well as everyday life in 1100, and additionally contains significant data regarding military engagements and tactics.

The Bayeux Tapestry had elicited world-wide praise and has especially captured the pride and respect of its "home town" admirers, those in Bayeux, Normandy, and Paris, France.

The Tillett Tapestry is a rainbow-hued "magic carpet" into the 16th century and the "new world" of our Western Hemisphere. This magic story about the arrival of the Spanish in Aztec Mexico appears on a 100-feet long, 33-inches wide single continuous hand-ground cotton cloth. It is multi-colored, embroidered with an estimated 55 million stitches, depicting 1,493 human figures and 741 non-human figures contained in 231 scenes. The borders contain 3,544 letters in bilingual text (Spanish along the top border; English along the bottom).

The work was researched, designed, and created by London-born Leslie Tillett, a renowned textile design master and authority on hand printing techniques, embroidery, and weaving. Conceived by Tillett, and encouraged by Diego Rivera, his research let to Aztec codices, Spanish records and data sources in museums, archives, and libraries, in Spain, Mexico, France, Austria, England and the United States.

Tillett completed hundreds of paintings from the originals in his Cuernavaca, Mexico gallery. He created the textile narrative by composing the individual scenes into a historical sequence, including the departure of Cortes from Cuba, his landing in what became Vera Cruz, and the battle for Tenochitilan, ending with the surrender of the last Aztec Emperor, Cuahtemoc, transferring the results to cloth in India ink.

The hand embroidery began in the early 1960s and was finally completed in 1977.

Tillett died in 1992. Doris "D.D." Tillett owned the tapestry until her death in Massachusetts in 2008. The husband and wife team served as consultants on handicraft product development to the governments of the Peoples' Republic of China, South Korea and Lesotho. They developed design projects for the American Indian Community through the School of the American Indians in New Mexico. They served as founding consultants on craft projects in emerging communities, such as the Printwork of Harlem, the Bed-Stuy Project, and the cathedral work of St. John the Devine.

Mr. Tillett's last 15 years were devoted to painting; he left a large body of work, including *Wind in the Buffalo Grass*; *African Art in Needlework*; *The Fall of the Aztecs*; *The Zoophabet*; *Needlework Book*; and the *Plant and animal Alphabet Coloring Book*.

I was asked why Mt. San Antonio College in southern California was chosen for the first showing of the Tillett Tapestry on the West Coast. I was a member of the college board of trustees and had agreed to serve as guest curator for this unique historic and artistic event.

I responded, citing four principal reasons. When my family and I first saw the tapestry during its 1982-1983 exhibitions at the *Instituto Cultural de Mexico* in San Antonio, Texas, we were overwhelmed by its beauty and the tremendous impact of its historical message. We carried the shining memory for some 15 years and decided to urge the Tilletts to permit a first exhibition on the West Coast, in an academic venue.

Second, we knew it had been exhibited at New York's Museum of Natural History, the Smithsonian, and in every major public art center in Mexico.

It was a unique opportunity to introduce one of the most remarkable women in the history of the Western Hemisphere. Doña Marina, was the cacica (a word the Spaniards brought from the Indies to describe the indigenous ruler of an area) of many towns and vassals, was a person of great importance throughout New Spain. She was known in Tlaxcala and Coatzacoalcos by the name of la Malinche, and was an incredible interpreter, negotiator and warrior, wife and mother, and the consort of Cortes.

No more fitting site existed for this exhibition than Mt. San Antonio College, a flagship educational institution located in Southern California's San Gabriel Valley, in the quiet college-oriented City of Walnut. The student body of some 42,000, with a major Hispanic component, is represented by a student association government which proposed to sponsor the event. Art Director Fatemeh Burnes is recognized for her masterful leadership in presenting significant art programs. There could be no finer venue for an educational presentation of this history-rich magnitude.

It is essential to understand the massive, decisive clash of cultures which has dominated the Western hemisphere since the Spanish arrival in Aztec Mexico.

Herewith is a brief review of unique essentials of each culture.

Spain defeated the Moors after years of bitter battle. Columbus "discovered" a new world; fabulous tales trumpeted by the popular, sensation-oriented publication *Amadis de Gaula* and similar "lying histories" produced a nation enthralled with dreams of El Dorado, Cibola, the Seven Enchanted Cities, the Fountain of Youth, and stories of gold, pearls and Amazons. (Some semanticists argue that the name of the U.S. state of California is derived from the *Amadis de Gaula* heroine Calidia, Queen of the Amazons, who commanded an aerial army of five hundred ferocious griffins.

Notions of chivalric armored knights abounded, to be later targeted in Miguel de Cervantes' 1605 masterpiece *Adventures of Don Quixote de la Mancha.*

A remarkable literary parallel is found in Nunez Cabeza de Vaca's letter to his king, describing the journey from Florida to the Pacific (1528 - 1536). In *Interlinear to Cabeza De Vaca* author Haniel Long described the expedition as one that led across the "steaming land," where de Vaca's party of 578 marched with glittering armor and horses "covered with gaudy trappings" towards utter ruin, in the belief that he would share in the "glory of Cortes and his murderous band."

In the main, inscribed monoliths, seals, Aztec codices, architectural remains, and engineering remnants such as irrigation channels and roadways reveal the socio-political and economic organizations reflecting the customs, habits, and work of the tribes and nations in Meso – America. At the time of the arrival of Spanish adventurers like Cortes, Grijalva, and Hernando de Cordova, perhaps a dozen linguistic families contained some 100 different languages in the area we now call Mexico.

Much before the arrival of the Spanish – perhaps the 12th century – tremendous cultural catastrophe often awkwardly compared with the fall of the Roman Empire had occurred in Meso-America, devastating civilizations, such as the Toltec and Mayan. However, magnificent monuments to the creative genius of those cultures remain. The renowned pyramids of the sun and moon (200 - 400 BC); Tula (Hildago); Palenque

(Chiapas); Edz Na (Camoeche); Codz-Kabah (Yucatan); Tulum (Quintana Roo); Mitla and Monte Alban (Oaxaca); and Chichen Itza (Yucatan). The Aztecs, the People of the Sun, were dominated by prophecies of imminent return of Quetzalcoatl, a cultural hero figure portending destruction and chaos of the Aztecs by their God, Huitzilopochtli.

Enter the Spanish adventurers, freebooters, pillagers, and murderers – newcomers stunned by what they saw, especially in the Valley of Anahuac and Lake Texcoco. Bernal Diaz described a scene as producing amazement at the sight of so many cities and villages and "that straight causeway" that led to Mexico City. "We were amazed," he wrote, comparing the land to "enchanted things related in the *Book of Amadis*" because of the huge towers, temples, and buildings rising up, all built of masonry. It was enough to prompt some of the soldiers to ask whether the sightings were produced in a dream.

The Tillett Tapestry brings more than the excitement of thousands of multi-colored embroidery stitches depicting the arrival of the Spanish in Aztec Mexico." The story through the weaving suggests a series of historical challenges and a daunting array of questions about cultures in conflict in our hemisphere.

Did the arrival and subsequent warfare constitute an uprising of Aztec-dominated tribes, a rebellion, a revolution, or subjugation by conquistadores? What is the real significance of the role of Cortes' interpreter, advisor, guide, warrior, and consort, the young woman named Malinche, and later described as Doña Marina? There are substantive reasons to believe Malinche was not a traitor. Instead, the woman was chosen to carry out the plans and hopes of the many tribes along the Gulf Coast who were angry at the ferocity and cruelty of the Aztecs who demanded annual tributes of food, animals, and women. The sinking of Cortes' ships at Vera Cruz prevented the Spanish troops from returning to Cuba or Spain, and subsequently Malinche led Cortes and his freebooters to Tenochtitlan to defeat the

Aztecs and loot the City of its riches. It forever removed the tribute-yoke of the Aztecs.

How do the tapestry's historical depictions impact Spanish-speaking citizens today? An indigenous leader rued the association of shame, poverty and, illiteracy with the culture of the indigenous. The Tillett Tapestry challenges this lamentable belief.

How do we relate the entire Spanish-Aztec conflict to that of the arrival of the English in the "new world" and the subsequent impacts on the Northern Indian Nations? How can the arrival be compared to a massive cultural upheaval such as the Australian experience with an aboriginal culture? How will the impact of the Columbus expedition upon the Arawak peoples in the Caribbean be evaluated?

I am convinced the Tillett Tapestry is alive with vigorous concepts, attitudes, and perspectives. It represents one of the finest teaching tools I have seen in this country, and goes to the heart of cultural confrontations. This conviction was reinforced when I watched thousands of students move through the art gallery presenting questions and comments.

The lectures in conjunction with the exhibition on language, economics, art, customs, music, architecture, and religion reinforced my belief that the Tillett Tapestry is a communicative medium of the largest order, a medium, a teaching tool, and a gem that should be travelling through high schools, colleges, and universities.

Currently, the Tillett Tapestry is in the custody of the Leslie Tillett family estate, which is contemplating sale of the tapestry to a museum for exhibition and educational purposes.

The Tapestry is a Western hemisphere treasure, a coruscant mirror-image of one of the most massive cultural impacts our hemisphere has sustained. It may well prove to be one of public education's most valuable teaching tools, as well as an integrative influence in Hispanic-Anglo relationships.

14

Public Libraries

Libraries have been in existence in the western world for close to five thousand years. They parallel the cultural state of western man from the Nile to the Hudson, from the Euphrates to the Amazon.
  —Elmer Johnson and Michael Harris:
  Histories of Libraries in the Western World

The word library is basically defined as a place set apart to contain books and other literary material for reading, study, or reference. It is derived from the Latin *librarium* = place to keep books.

For me, a "place set apart" has a special meaning and importance that I have found in our competitive, aggressive and often frenetic culture in two places: public libraries and churches. Years ago, when working in the heart of downtown Los Angeles, I would often forgo lunch and walk to the old public square where the mission *Nuestra Señora, Reina de Ciudad de Los Angeles* is located. I went to the mission during times of special stress, times of disappointment or doubt. I sat in the sometimes empty mission, a building old and venerated as the recipient of sorrows, hopes, and joys. It is a place experienced in caring. I went to rest, to be healed by the peace which the building itself offered.

I have often found a comparable feeling when I walk into a public library. It is, to me, the caring representative of our culture holding treasures of communication. I go into libraries for support. I go for ideas, for encouragement, certitude, and pragmatism conjoined with vast perspectives.

Both realms, the public library and the old mission, hold for me the answer to the question posed by Job:

"But where shall wisdom be found? And where is the place of understanding?" (*Job* 28-12).

There can be little doubt that history and culture offer an answer: public libraries and venerable religious structures.

In ancient Egypt, Babylon, and Assyria; in Greece and Rome, libraries constituted and preserved the culture, whether for the special few as in Egypt, or for the many in the Roman Imperium, where libraries developed into government-financed institutions, free and open to the public. In the Moslem world, library centers flourished in Damascus, Bagdad, Cairo, and Cordoba. It has been established that books in private hands (1200 AD) exceeded the total of all libraries, public and private, in Western Europe.

It has been noted that in the world of libraries, including religious, governmental, business records, archives, and those of private families, whether involving such print media as clay, tablets, papyrus or parchment, the arrival of the printing press was an event of enormous impact and singular importance.

The entire concept and process of libraries was affected, especially in Western Europe where countless thousands of monks worked at desks in monasteries copying and recopying old parchments that they barely understood. They seldom added to them, or extracted any ideas from them.

It is astonishing that one man, Johann Gutenberg, could turn the world upside down, somewhat in the fashion that automobiles displaced horses in the world of transport.

Gutenberg produced the monumental 42-line Bible pages, an exquisite masterpiece printed on six presses simultaneously. In one copy a hand-lettered rubrication appeared: "August 24, 1450."

Other works attributed to Gutenberg include *Poem on the Last Judgment*, a Latin grammar, four calendars, and an encyclopedic dictionary that contained an imprint of 1460 and the statement: "With the protection of the All-highest, Who reveals to the humble what he conceals to the wise."

And so it was that the self-styled "humble one" effectively wiped out the occupation of thousands upon thousands of scribes and librarians, by effectively creating and introducing a simple, direct, practical, and swift medium for communication via mechanical printing. The origin of libraries as a "place set apart" in early America was beset with struggle.

The Rev. John Milban noted that "man must have bread before books. Men must build barns before they establish colleges." Nonetheless, the 1850s saw the recognition, definition and support of public libraries as necessary concomitants to public education.

It is generally agreed that the trustees of the Boston Public Library issued a seminal report concerning the need for substantial library services throughout the country. The report was especially directed to the need for establishment of a public library service system in Boston. Its analysis and conclusions are deemed to be nationally applicable, in that "reading ought to be furnished to all, as a matter of public policy and duty." The report indicated that libraries should be furnished on the same principle as that of free education, and that it is of "paramount importance" to diffuse to the greatest number of persons such information that may be understood as educational.

Based upon wide public support for these concepts, the Boston Public Library opened in 1854.

Three landmarks in the increasing recognition of the importance of libraries in America are acknowledged: the creation of the American Library Association at Philadelphia, the report on public libraries in the United States and the establishment of the *Library Journal*, and the funding provided for library creation in both the U.S. and the United Kingdom.

Andrew Carnegie is recognized as history's greatest library benefactor. He funded some 2,500 buildings, constructed with personal donations of approximately $50,000,000.

A few comments about Andrew Carnegie are appropriate. His vision of the life of a rich man was described in his essay "The Gospel of Wealth," in which he explained that "the rich mans life should fall into two periods: first, that of acquiring wealth," followed by the distribution of it in a manner "that the surplus would be used for the general Welfare." His success in forming the U.S. Steel Corporation made enemies, made evident in 1901 when he offered the city of Detroit $750,000 contingent upon the city adding $500,000. Detroit declined his "tainted money" because of public opposition until 10 years later.

On the college and university scene, Harvard, Yale, Princeton, University of Pennsylvania, Columbia, Brown University, Cornell, Dartmouth, Rutgers, Georgetown, and three State Universities in Virginia, North Carolina and the University of Texas were among the country's major education institutions providing extensive library services. Midwestern universities including Chicago, Michigan, Minnesota and Illinois are frontrunners as well.

Librarial progress presented interesting problems in the Virginia colony of 1620. Collections of books were sent from England to assist in establishing a library for an institution to be called "Henrico Indian College." This enterprise was abandoned because of the Indian Uprising of 1622. In consequence, it was not until 1693 that William and Mary College was founded. Much later, the University of Virginia became prominent. Thomas Jefferson, who designed the university's rotunda, led the efforts to bring its library to national prominence.

Jefferson is the principal in one of history's most curious footnotes regarding the provision of books for special public purposes. It was Jefferson's concern that "a simple account of Jesus" be produced in a form suited to the comprehension of the American Indians. This was probably a reaction to difficulties previously encountered with indigenous Americans.

The first version Jefferson contemplated was to be called "The Philosophy of Jesus of Nazareth" and would be an abridgement of the New Testament. It was a years-long self-imposed project that he admitted was performed for his own use "by cutting verse by verse out of the printed book" and arranging it into an "octavo of forty-six pages of pure and unsophisticated doctrines, such as were professed and acted upon by the unlettered Apostles, the Apostolic Fathers, and the Christians of the first Century."

This abridgement of the New Testament was published and presented to the United States Congress on May 13, 1802. 9,000 copies were delivered to the Senate and 600 went to the House. The project might well have been anticipated in a May 15, 1819 letter from Jefferson to Thomas Parke.

"Were I to be the founder of a new sect," wrote Jefferson, "I would call them Apiarians and, after the example of the bee, advise them to extract the honey from every sect."

Authors Elmer D. Johnson and Michael H. Harris have produced a magnificent record in their *History of Libraries in the Western World*. It is a "push-button war" they write, that may be started in seconds and ended only through years of patient effort. "Books and libraries can play a most important role in this effort toward world peace and toward arousing the people of the world to fight ignorance, intolerance, disease, and poverty instead of each other." The authors note that books and libraries are significant contributors to the rise of western civilization.

In the years 2002, 2003, and 2004, libraries throughout the United States have suffered from decreasing financial support at both private and city-state levels. This decline has been attributed by many officials to budget crises caused by plummeting sales tax revenues, sky-rocketing healthcare costs, and government workers' retiree plans. As a result, library hours have been cut by 50% in many cities. Consequently, library services are jeopardized by budget cuts. It is reported that such services in Denver, Detroit, Lancaster PA, and Crawford County, OH, have slashed service hours. Entire branches of library systems have been closed. Erie County, in western New York State, is considering closure of its 52 public libraries unless the county's funding crisis is solved.

An interesting example of librarial distress is that of Salinas, California's John Steinbeck Library. It serves as a memorial to the author of *Grapes of Wrath* and *Of Mice and Men*. Because of a $9 million shortfall, the city has proposed that all three of its public libraries be closed. Such a decision would place Salinas as one of the largest U.S. cities without library service. Steinbeck received the Nobel Prize for Literature in 1962.

It is reported that since 2002, library funding cuts in the U.S. have reached $900 million. 2,100 jobs have been eliminated, and 31 libraries closed. Such draconian measures stab at the heart of education. Research illuminates the fact that library quality is related to reading scores. Reports note that California has the worst school libraries in the country and ranks near the bottom in the quality of public libraries.

The State of California, the 7th largest economic engine in the world!

15

Communications

In all this Cuban business there is one man that stands out on the horizon of my memory like Mars at perihelion.
—Elbert Green Hubbard

It was at the public library at Ocean View, Virginia that I first read the above-quoted introductory statement in Elbert Hubbard's classic *A Message To Garcia*.

As a youngster about sixth-grade, the strange word "perihelion" caught my eye and captivated me sufficiently to read the brief story that followed.

The story has stayed with me for decades. The message was short, powerful, and direct. It contained an electricity that was intense and inspiring. It received nationwide acclaim.

Simply, it is Hubbard's magnificent story of a war going on between Spain and the United States. Cuba was the principal stage. It became urgent that President McKinley communicate with Garcia, the leader of the insurgents who was somewhere in the Cuban Jungle.

How to find him?

One of the president's advisers suggested "a fellow by the name of Rowan will find Garcia for you, if anyone can."

Garcia was chosen to deliver the message, a task that all knew was exceedingly dangerous and almost unbelievably difficult to achieve.

Rowan did not hesitate in accepting the responsibility; his country called; he proceeded without equivocation, without hesitance, and, as author Hubbard describes, Rowan set off.

He reached the huge island of Cuba in four days and waded ashore from the open boat, then worked his way through jungle territory. Three weeks later Rowan emerged on the far side of the island, having "traversed a hostile country on foot, and delivered his letter to Garcia."

Hubbard's point: McKinley gave Rowan the task of delivering a letter. Rowan did not hesitate, and accomplished the mission of responsibility imposed upon him. Rowan was a hero!

Through grade school, high school and college that story did not fade away. What an example, I often thought, of bravery and commitment! Rowan's dauntless action and achievement was a model to be emulated!

It was not until years later I awakened with an image-shock. Was there more to this story, this achievement? Were there lessons about "message" – about communication? What if the message to be delivered had been handed, ultimately and successfully, to the insurgent leader Garcia, who, upon its opening, discovers it to be written in Greek, a language neither Rowan nor Garcia understood? All that bravery, brought to naught because the message, the "communication," was not understandable? Consider an alternative: What if Garcia the insurgent was a heavily bearded man (very likely in a jungle environment) and opened the message only to read: "Use Burma Shave?"

These questions go to the heart of "communication." To be effective, the message must be (a) understandable and (b) relevant. True, there is a great deal more to communication than that, but these constitute basic starting points, the ineluctable necessity for effectiveness.

There are other factors, often neglected, in addition to delivery, such as value norms of both sender and receiver. It a lesson often evident at Christmas time as observed in the beautifully-wrapped present enclosing a nondescript gift.

Elbert Green Hubbard (1856 - 1915) was an author, editor, and publisher. He founded Roycroft Press in East Aurora, New York and gained fame with his monthly publication, and *Little Journey* books. He published *The Philistine*, an *avant-garde* magazine, and it was in this publication that his masterpiece "A Message to Garcia" appeared in 1889. Hubbard died in the sinking of the cruise ship Lusitania, on May 7, 1915.

I am indebted to author Hubbard not only because he encouraged me to look up the word "perihelion" (from the Greek *peri* + *helios*; nearest the sun) but also because his story about Rowan forced me to respect the semantics involved in the word "communication" (from the Latin *co* + *minus*; to share with another, e.g., gift, service). Also, the several meanings attributed to "communication" in dictionary definitions serve as a reminder that many words are "portmanteau words" carrying one or more meanings. This is especially evident in this example dictionary definition of "communication" for example:

- to give to another as a partaker
- to impart, transmit
- to administer the Eucharist

One of the most unique affirmations of the power of communication is "Gift of the Magi" by the short story master, O. Henry (William Sydney Porter). Reduced to its essentials, it is the story of Della and Jim, who struggle to survive desperate economic circumstances. It is the day before Christmas. Della has too little money to buy Jim a present and decides to sell her greatest asset: her long hair. (It reached below her knee and made itself almost a garment for her.) She sold her hair to a collector for $20, enough money to buy her Jim a beautiful platinum fob for his prized possession – a watch. Now, Christmas would be wonderful! When Jim arrives home she shows him the gift and it takes it in stunned silence. Finally, he says, "Look what I've bought for you – the hair comb you wanted, the pure tortoiseshell with jewel rims. I sold the watch to buy your comb. Let's put our presents away. They're too nice to use..."

The author concludes: "Let it be said that of all who give gifts, these two were the wisest of all who give and receive, they are the Magi.

O. Henry, the penname of William Sydney Porter, died in New York on June 5, 1910. His last words: "Turn up the lights; I don't want to go home in the dark". There is a beautiful memorial in Greensboro, North Carolina, honoring O. Henry. It is a statue containing a large, open book. A little boy peers from behind a page.

Communication is the oil in the engine of relationships. Communities and cultures are derived from every contact, from every event within the web of never-ceasing relationships.

From the casual, *pro forma* "Good Morning"! How are you?" the communication process is automatically at work. The query "How are YOU?" is seldom a serious interest in the other's health. Indeed, we are not inviting a reply citing aches and pains. Similarly, the response "Fine!" is usually devoid of health-orientation. Then, what is the exchange about? Perhaps it is simply to prove we are here and alive, to be reassured of our presence. And, "fine" usually posits the subterranean assurance of "Me too!"

Do you remember the words in poet Robert Browning's "Pippa Passes?" As the little girl skips through a small village early in a beautiful morning, she sings "God's in his Heaven, all's right with the world!" Pippa is vital, youthful; her message radiant. At that moment, the words shine like gold, the song floats gently; indeed, God's in His Heaven. Surely, for a blessed moment, all is all right with the world!

"In the beginning was the Word," – John 1:1.

"How forcible are right words!" – Job 6:25.

"There is no calamity which right words will not redress." – Ralph Waldo Emerson.

Words. Each word reflects the cumulative wisdom of the culture. Many words have a history of thousands of years. A good dictionary is a treasure, housing communicative symbols and gems. Hence, the title "thesaurus" (from Greek = treasure).

Currently, scholars concerned with historical linguistics contend that the base or origin of English, Latin, and Sanskrit emerged from Indo-European languages some 8,000 - 9,000 years ago, moving from Turkey into Europe. Two New Zealand biologists are advancing the concept that languages have "foot words" with patterns of similarity that might be considered comparable to the DNA analyses which posit relationships between animal groups.

Here follows a quick look at a few words which – like people – are unique.

Vaudeville: in the U.S., the word describes a form of (sometimes raucous) stage entertainment featuring singing, dancing, and comedy routines. Its origin comes from the French *Chansons du Vau Vire* a song of the Valley of Vire in Normandy.

Ouija: a board with letters of the alphabet, over which a small 3-legged device slides while fingers of the participants rest upon the moving device. It is employed to gather "answers." It is composed of two words: "OUI" (French) and "JA" (German), and that both words mean "YES!"

Nova: from Latin *novus* = new, but translates literally in Spanish as *no va* = no go!

Judo: A Japanese word composed of characters that mean "gentle" and "way" – the "gentle way," but Judo does not confine itself to gentleness.

Serendipity: This word emerged in a letter Horace Walpole sent to Horace Mann in 1754. Walpole wrote: "I once read a silly fairy tale," and described the story of the *Three Princes of Serendip* in which the royalty traveled and were always making discoveries by accident and sagacity. One of their unexpected discoveries was a mirror called the "Mirror of Justice." If one faced the mirror and spoke untruthfully, the mirrored face would become black, while the image of a truthful person would retain its natural image. Hence, the mirror's power made no witness necessary. In that way, and in view of the special virtue of the mirror, it was possible in this land to live a quiet and peaceful life.

The mirror – what a communicator!

It is important to realize that many words may inherit double, or treble communicative responsibilities and definitions. It was this context that Lewis Carroll's Humpty Dumpty outlined to Alice (through the looking glass) the definition of a "portmanteau" word.

"You see," he explained, "it's like a portmanteau. There are two meanings packed up into one word." Portmanteau words have become commonplace in words that are packed with more than one meaning in the fashion of a suitcase, or its vintage equivalent, the portmanteau.

Words and phrases are sometimes extracted from mythology and sometimes from real people." For example, Terminus was the ancient god of landmarks. His statue was a stone post set in the ground to mark boundaries of fields. Today, we describe ending positions as "terminal points."

Thomas Hobson was an English liveryman who died in 1621, who required his customers to take the next available horse rather than give them a choice. "Hobson's choice" is no choice at all.

Charles C. Boycott (1824 - 1898) was a farm manager who infuriated his Irish tenants. They organized a "land league" and refused to harvest crops on any land managed by Boycott. They were incensed because he refused to lower rents.

A series of lines carefully painted on merchant ships to indicate depths to which ships can be safely loaded was the creation of Samuel J. Plimsoll (1821 - 1898), a member of the British Parliament who caused legislation to be passed to achieve maritime safety.

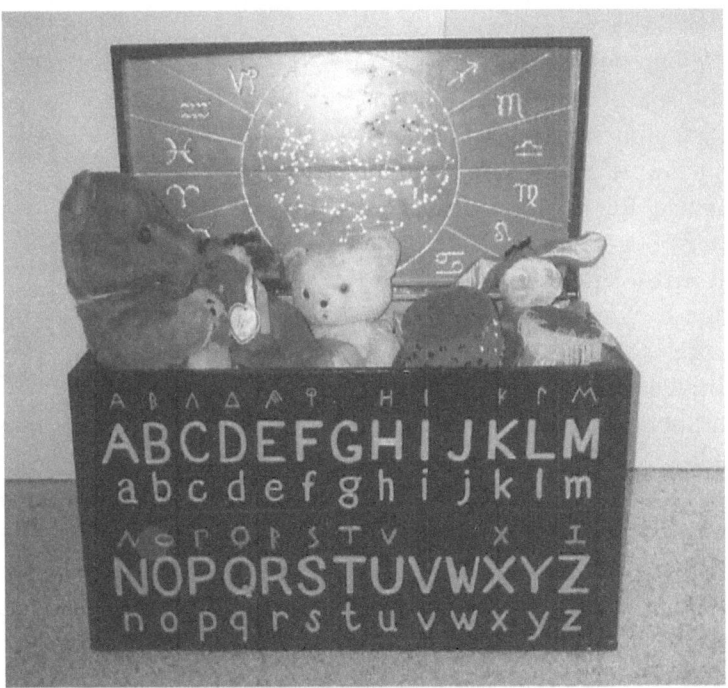

The Magic Box

Words are the children of alphabets. These "children" can be transmitted by the simplest devices of symbolism, Morse code, Braille, or semaphore. Samuel Finley Morse (1791 - 1872) is well-known in the U.S. for his accomplishment in the field of communication. He conceived the idea of a single-current electromagnetic telegraph with an alphabet in dots and dashes. It came to be termed the Morse code. In 1843, the U.S. Congress voted to pay Morse to build the first telegraph line in the country, running from Baltimore to Washington. In 1844, he sent his first message: "What hath God wrought?"

Morse was one of the first practitioners with the early daguerreotype photographic method. He was often in court to protect his telegraphic invention. The U.S. Supreme Court held in his favor in 1854.

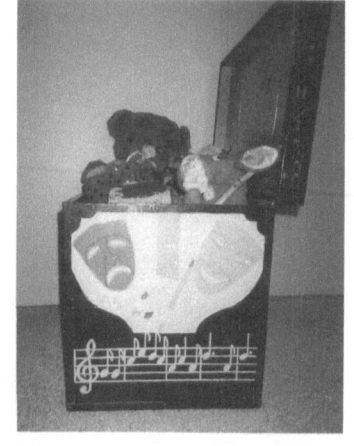

Louis Braille (1809 - 1852) was born in France, and while playing in his father's shop at the age of three, was blinded by a falling knife. While it was Valentine Hauy who discovered that blind persons could decipher texts in embossed Roman letters, it was Braille at age 15 who worked out a system with six dots, now termed a Braille cell. The dots are numbered 1, 2, 3 on the left side and 4, 5, 6 on the right, and allow the blind to see words on a page. Braille was also noted as a talented organist and he extended his system to musical notations.

Semaphore comes from the Greek *sema* = sign + *phoros* = bearing, and is a system of communication generally employing flags.

Our communication is inextricably interwoven with our information process. Peter F. Drucker, in his masterful 1998 *The Next Information Revolution*, drives home the long process, which began with the invention of writing in Mesopotamia, some 5,000 - 6,000 years ago, followed perhaps 1,000 years later in China, and some 1,500 years later in our Western hemisphere as found in the Mayan Culture. The invention of the written book is believed to have occurred in China first about 1,300 BC and Greece about 800 years later. As a final component to the communications change, Gutenberg's invention of the printing press about 1450 forever changed the information process. Most of these efforts dealt with creating and preserving information.

Drucker emphasized the great turning point in the tasks of creating and preserving information. A new, vast realm was opened in speedy communication. He contends that printing made the Protestant reformation possible, when Luther nailed his 95 theses to a church door in an obscure German town. These were immediately printed and distributed, gratis, all over Europe. The leaflets ignited the religious firestorm that turned into the Reformation.

When I was quite young, my father told me about a magical box, a box that contained the secrets of the world. I asked, often, what was in the box. He would say, "When you are a little older, I'll tell you all about it!"

That "little older" time finally arrived. He said, "When the magic box is opened, you will see the letters of the alphabet, the numbers 1 through 9, and the Zero. With these, you can learn, you can achieve, you can understand other people and they can understand you. These are the magical building blocks of civilized people."

During that experience, I think my father also shared with me the story of the Ancient Greeks: Pandora, who was given marriage blessing gifts in a beautiful box. When she opened it, all the blessings escaped except Hope, the most precious of all the gifts! He said the magic box he had told me about, with alphabet, numbers, and zero, represented the present day concept of Hope for mankind.

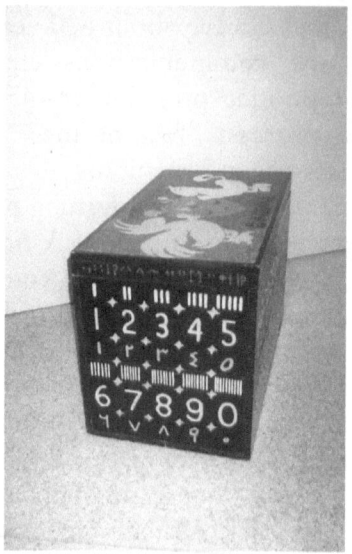

The Magic Box of Secrets

There came a day when I wanted to tell my son about the magic box and the great secrets. My memory was very clear about my father's story, but I felt that memory was all I had about that long-ago occasion. I decided to bring the magic box into reality – visually and physically – into my son's life.

I created a large, wooden box, large enough to hold many toys.

It turned into a project 3 feet long, 26 inches wide, and 2 feet deep, composed of soft pine boards ½ inch thick. The covering lid was 2 and ½ inches deep, and the box 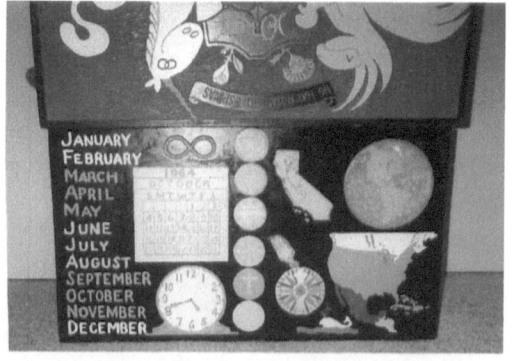 rested upon four casters for easy moving. There were carvings, 1/4 inch deep, on all four sides and top, exhibiting the symbols of communication: alphabet (caps and lower case); numbers ("stick", Arabic); music; drama; geography; and symbols of major religions. The top depicted a heraldic scene of armorial bearings: a chicken with a thistle and a unicorn with a rose, to illustrate the heraldic message: *No Hay Rosas Sin Espinas* or "There are no roses without thorns". The back of the box was carved with data concerning the date, day, time, and place of my son's birth. The inside of the box cover depicts signs of the Zodiac and constellations at the time of his birth.

The inclusion of the unicorn has raised questions. I have generally defended its presence by referring to Carroll's *Through the Looking Glass* wherein the unicorn says to Alice "talk, child," to which Alice replies, "Do you know, I always thought unicorns were fabulous monsters. I never saw one alive before!" The unicorn responds, "Well, now that we have seen each other, if you'll believe in me, I'll believe in you." What priceless pearls are contained in the unicorn's statement. Pearls of communicative wisdom, understanding, compassion, and acceptance!

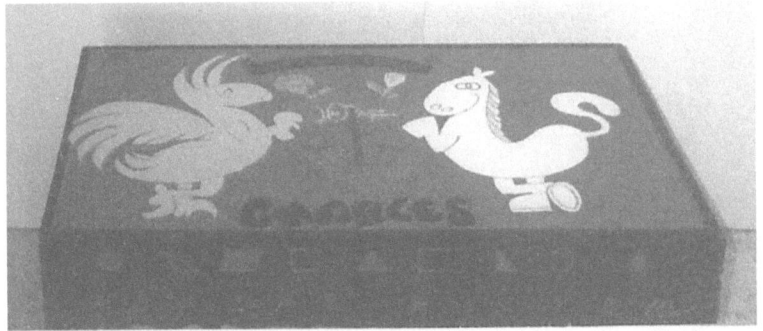

The Magic Box: Heraldic Design

Whether the mythology of Pandora's wedding box, the *pragma* of delivering a message to Garcia, the passionate exchange in *Gifts of the Magi*, the song of Pippa Passes, the serendipitous discoveries of Morse, Braille, and Gutenberg, or the construction of a toy box covered with magic symbols

– the omnipresent necessity of effective communication remains.

At a small Peruvian town in the Sacred Valley of the Incas, we saw small groups of young men enjoying lunch at an outdoor vendor's stall. Before drinking, they would pour a small portion of the contents on the ground, while saying, softly, *pacha Mama*. These sons of the Incas were saying, in Quecjua, "Thank you, Mother Earth." It is a part of their relationship to the earth and their universe. It is a consummate commentary on the ultimate significance of communication.

16

Catastrophism

*Where wast thou when I laid the foundations of the
earth?.*
—the Book of Job

According to Biblical literature, the above quotation
initiates the Lord's response to a series of angry
questions hurled at Him by Job, a distraught man
who feels mistreated, humiliated, punished and abandoned by
his Maker.

Further, Job was asked, "Whereupon are the foundations
thereof fastened, or who laid the cornerstone thereof?" In a
brilliant, challenging analysis entitled "Answer to Job", Carl
Gustav Jung states, "The Book of Job is a landmark in the
long historical development of a divine drama."

This commentary about catastrophism involves the
foundations of the earth and two mammoth asteroids or
meteorites that smashed into our Water Planet. The
geological definition of catastrophism is that doctrine in
which certain vast geological changes in the world's history
were caused by cataclysm rather than gradual evolutionary
processes. Whether catastrophe (from Greek "over turning")

or cataclysm (Greek "deluge"), the Greeks intuited the Ultimate, the End.

Originally, Earth was "all together." Some name the "first" earth-mass Pangea. It is premised that about 200 million years ago the Triassic era introduced a "breakup" that separated Pangea into two great north-south land masses.

The breakup was presumably caused by the shifting of massive tectonic plates which float upon a soft undergirding mantle. This mantle may have been the subject of the Lord's reference to Earth's "foundations" and "corner stone."

Then – 135 million years later – another breakup occurred, possibly caused by the shifting plates. This was followed by a third breakup that introduced the Cretaceous Age about 65 million years ago. Today's Earth configuration gives us the resultant North and South American hemispheres, Africa, Asia, Australia, the Arctic and Antarctic, etc.

Why this revue of Earth's "Great Breakings?" Essentially, to ponder Job's plight. Harassed and seemingly abandoned by an Almighty presence, how could Job possibly respond effectively about the foundations of the Earth? How could he explain how they were "fastened?" How, who, or what laid the Earth's cornerstone?

It is instructive to extend Job's questioning and additionally discuss two massive impacts by hurtling asteroids or meteorites on Earth eons ago. Scientists have learned much about Earth's foundations and how they are supported, shift, and determine new continental configurations. They recognize that plates may shift horizontally and they may rise or fall vertically.

Because of research into land-mass changes, it is understandable that theories abound about "lost" land masses. Hence, the intriguing stories about Atlantis, MU and a series of lesser "islands." The ancient Greeks had a fable about the "fortunate islands" located somewhere in the Western Ocean, which gave birth to the legend of the "Happy Island of Atlantis."

What about the two great asteroid or meteorite impacts? When and where did they occur? Job, when being aggressively quizzed by the Lord about the foundations was asked, "Who hath laid the measures thereof, if thou knowest? Or who hath stretched the line upon it?"

It may be comforting, if suddenly pressed by a Powerful Interrogator, at least to have a few facts about such matters as tectonic plates, mantles, and two extraordinary "impacts." Scientists concerned about the disappearance of dinosaurs some 65 million years ago, believe an asteroid some six miles in diameter crashed into Earth at that time off the Yucatan Peninsula of Mexico. It created a gigantic crater now called Chicxulub which – after its inundation – we identify as the Gulf of Mexico. This gigantic impact caused the extinction of dinosaurs and a host of other species.

An excellent summary of these events, and a concomitant review of theories about the star "Nemesis," "Planet X," and the 26-million-years cycle of Earth-impacting asteroids may be found in the guidebook *Dinosaurs*, by Jay Stevenson and George McGhee.

A 2004 discovery produced substantial evidence pointing to the greatest extinction event in Earth's history about 250 million years ago. The evidence is a crater located off the northwestern coast of Australia. Geological researchers from the University of California at Santa Barbara, paleobiologists from the Museum of Natural History in Washington D.C.), NASA astrobiologists, and geochemists from the University of Rochester are reported to believe the 125 mile crater is the result of a massive impact during the time of the boundary formation between the Permian and Triassic Periods.

We are more fortunate than Job. When confronted by the Almighty regarding "foundations" and "measurements" of this planet, we might respond with a few relevant answers. For example, Earth's crust varies in thickness from 3 to 30 miles. The foundation of the crust is a rock layer called the mantle which is about 1,800 miles thick.

A present-day Job would also be able to present a description of attacks upon the Earth's foundations. In addition to the vast impacts of shifting tectonic plates some 200 million years ago, and again 155 million years later, the two asteroids or meteorites that smashed into the Earth caused enormous damage to animal and plant life.

Of course, there have been other impacts such as the one causing the Siberian Crater, the impact creating the Chesapeake Bay, the Manicouaga Crater of Quebec, the Arizona Crater; and the Stony Tunguska.

When will the next massive tectonic shift occur or the mammoth meteorite or asteroid strike?

There are those who predict our population growth might well swell to such an extent that by the year 2600 there will be less than one square yard of the Earth's surface available to each person. Could it be that these measurements might encourage another vast tectonic shift or another monstrous "extinction" meteorite?

Another view is that contained in John Van Auden's "Science's Mythology," in *Ancient Mysteries,* published by the Association for Research and Enlightenment. Van Auden contends that the Earth will find its way back to Pangea once again and humanity will return to its original brotherhood and sisterhood.

Why not embrace this beneficent concept? After all, Job was finally relieved of his unfairly-imposed burdens, restored to his former high status, and embraced again by the Almighty. If, indeed, the Book of Job constitutes a landmark that historically depicts the unfolding of a "divine drama," we can accept our roles as *dramatis personae* who understand the power of Brotherhood and Sisterhood.

17

Scouting

*With the exception of great religious and political
ideologies, no international organization has exerted a
greater influence upon social behavior than Boy and Girl
Scouts.*
  −*Tim Jeal,* The Boy Man: the Life of Lord
Baden-Powell

Memories of Boy Scout Troop #18 in Ocean View,
Virginia, compel the dedication of this chapter,
especially for the four major guideposts the Boy
Scouts of America offered and emphasized: Oath, Law,
Motto, and Slogan. These four defined scoutings were
impressive, understandable, important, respected — and
committed to memory.

Because of the remarkable similitude between the Boys
Scouts of America, and the Girl Scouts of the USA
(founding dates: BSA-1910; GSUSA-1912), and interrelated
cooperative leadership between Lord Baden-Powell and
Juliette Gordon Low, their organizational structures including
insignia, merit and proficiency badges, scouting levels,

national and world conferences, and fundamental scouting pledges and promises, I am convinced it is reasonable to express my appreciation – indeed, my debt – to the worldwide movement of scouting. My days in scouting gave me more than pleasant memories. Scouting described and defined citizenship goals. Scouting provided avenues to reach these goals. Constructive encouragement was omnipresent: Be Prepared anticipated the challenges and opportunities of life.

It is estimated that the scouting movement worldwide has involved more than 500 million members in more than 150 countries.

| Boy Scouts of America | 25 million members |
| Girl Scouts of the USA | 10 million members |

SCOUTING: CONCEPTUAL BASIS

- Non-military
- Non political
- Inter-denominational
- Inter-racial

Scouting was not permitted during three regimes: Fascist Italy, Germany, or Communist rule.

It is generally agreed that Lord Baden-Powell of Gilwell, England, a decorated soldier celebrated for his successful defense of the besieged South African town of Mafeking during the Boer War, is the Founder of the scouting movement.

The Boer War was declared October 11, 1899. 9,000 armed Boers moved on the small town of Mafeking. According to E. E. Reynolds, author of the extensively-documented book *Baden-Powell*, the population of Mafeking at the time of the 217 day siege consisted of some 1,000 white and 8,000 natives.

Famous for his successful resistance and leadership during the siege, "B.P." returned to England as a national hero and devoted his energies to defining and creating the scouting movement. His *Scouting for Boys* was enthusiastically received.

Lord Baden-Powell authored 33 books, received 17 orders and decorations, and was the recipient of 6 honorary degrees.

A Memorial Plaque in Westminster Abbey contains this simple tribute:

In Memory of
Robert Baden-Powell
Chief Scout of the World
1857- - -1941

Born in Savannah, Georgia, Juliette Low was called Daisy by friends and family. In 1886, she married William Low and they moved to England. Her husband died in 1906, and five years later she met Robert Baden-Powell and became interested in his scouting program.

In March 1912, Juliette Low returned to the U.S. with Baden-Powell's ideas and enthusiasm. Within days, a 16-page *Guides' Law* book was published containing the core of Baden-Powell's organizational structure and concepts. Almost overnight, patrols were organized in Savannah.

Juliette Low traveled back and forth between England and the U.S., encouraging and promoting the concept of Girl Scouts in the United States.

Washington D.C. was chosen for the National Office, and Low served as national president from 1915 to 1920. Juliette Low died January 17, 1927. Among her many honors: the issuance of a commemorative postage stamp, a liberty ship was named for her, she was installed in the Women's Hall of Fame at Seneca Falls, NY, and a Federal building in Savannah GA bears her name. A paragraph in *Girl Scout Collectors' Guide* describes Juliette Low's organization of the world's largest voluntary organization for girls, a group that has "influenced the lives of more than 10 million girls and adults who have been Girl Scouts."

BOY SCOUTS OF AMERICA

OATH - - MOTTO - - SLOGAN - - LAW
© 2004 Boy Scouts of America
Reprinted by permission

OATH

On my honor, I will do my best
To do my duty to God and my country
and to obey the Scout Law;
To help other people at all times;
To keep myself physically strong
mentally awake, and morally straight.

MOTTO

The Scout Motto is Be Prepared.
A Scout prepares for whatever comes
his way by learning all he can.
He keeps himself physically strong, healthy,
and ready to meet the challenges of life.

SLOGAN

The Scout slogan is Do A Good Turn Daily. Good turns are helpful acts of kindness, done quietly, without boasting, and without expecting reward or pay. Doing at least one Good Turn every day is a normal part of a Scout's life.

LAW. A SCOUT IS:

TRUSTWORTHY. A Scout tells the truth. He keeps promises. Honesty is a part of his code of conduct. People can always depend on him.

LOYAL. A Scout is true to his family, friends, Scout Leaders, school, nation and world community.

HELPFUL. A Scout is concerned about other people. He willingly volunteers to help others without expecting payment or reward.

FRIENDLY. A Scout is a friend to all. He is a brother to other Scouts. He seeks to understand others. He respects those with ideas and customs that are different from his own.

COURTEOUS. A Scout is polite to everyone regardless of age or position. He knows that good manners make it easier for people to get along together.

KIND. A Scout understands there is strength in being gentle. He treats others as he wants to be treated. He does not harm or kill anything without reason.

OBEDIENT. A Scout follows the rules of his family, school, and troop. He obeys the law of his community and country. If he thinks these rules and laws are unfair, he tries to have them changed in an orderly manner rather than disobey them.

CHEERFUL. A Scout looks for the bright side of life. He cheerfully does tasks that come his way. He tries to make others happy.

THRIFTY. A Scout works to pay his way and to help others. He saves for the future. He protects and conserves natural resources. He carefully uses time and property.

BRAVE. A Scout can face danger even if he is afraid. He has to courage to stand for what he thinks is right even if others laugh at him or threaten him.

CLEAN. A Scout keeps his body and mind fit and clean. He goes around with those who believe in living by these same ideals. He helps keep his home and community clean.

REVERENT. A Scout is reverent toward God. He is faithful in his religious duties. He respects the beliefs of others.

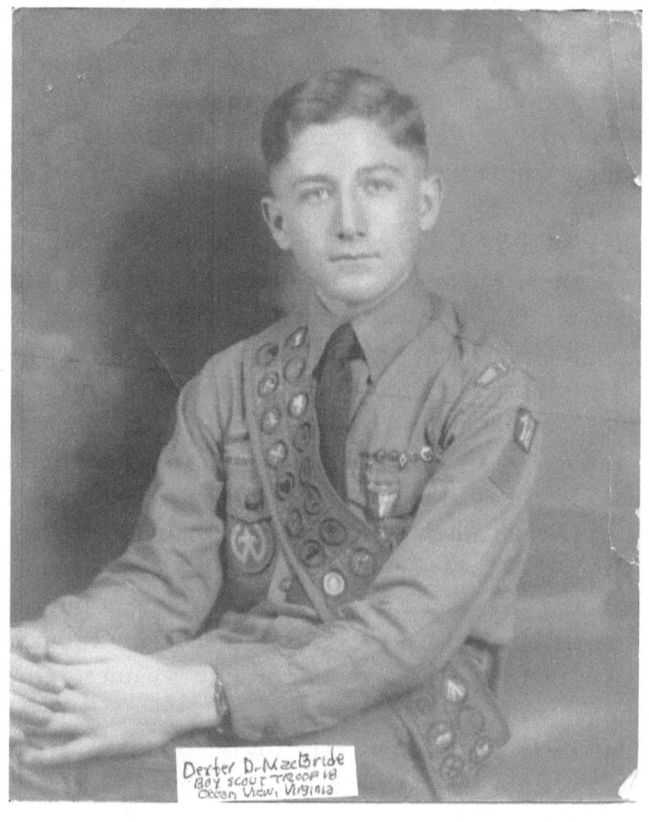

The author as an Eagle Scout, Ocean View Troop 18, Norfolk, Virginia (Circa 1929 - 1930)

18

Eminent Domain, Condemnation, Blight, Home

*Every man's home is his castle; even though the winds of
heaven man blow through it, the King of England cannot
enter it.*
   —Common Law maxim.

On the Fourth of July 2004, edition of the CBS
television program *60 Minutes,* considerable attention
was devoted to what was termed a "war" going on
in the City of Lakewood, Ohio (population of some 55,000).

The war centered upon a neighborhood of well-kept older
homes reflecting ownership pride, located on a very favorable
hillside site with an extensive, attractive view. City officials, in
search of increased revenues, decided the site would be better
utilized for high-rise apartments and high-paying business
shops.

The city condemned the housed by declaring them to be
"blighted." The homeowners fought condemnation process
but claimed to be losing because the court system may be
viewing the city's taking under the claim of blight as proper.

Later, the citizens of Lakewood voted against the proposal.

Take a big breath – city governments all over the U.S. are considering such takings as a way to improve their city. The idea is to take the citizens' properties, pay what is termed "just compensation according to the law" (in the Ohio case, get the long-time resident homeowners out of the way), at which point the City can then sell or transfer the area to other private parties who will "build up" the area. The guise is the creation of profitable businesses or high-rise apartments that might generate much higher taxes for the city than the former homeowners were paying.

The city, while admitting the houses are not "blighted" (they meet all the City laws, maintenance requirements, etc.), defended its preemptive action over the "need the money. We will ultimately improve the area. It is a matter of progress for the city." Officials claimed eminent domain with intent to pay the homeowners 'just compensation."

If you are thoughtful, informed, and awake, doesn't the idea of "just compensation" strike you as odd? Consider the fact that "just compensation" is measured and doled out as of the time of the taking. Hence, the owner if a $200,000 home or site must be paid the amount determined as of the date of the taking. But, PRESTO! The day after the taking is consummated and the $200,000 "fair market value" award is paid to the homeowner, that very same property – the land itself – may now be worth $1,000,000. Surely, if the city fights so hard to condemn and take the property it does so because the property will be worth many times the erstwhile $200,000. The real value of the property, so adamantly sought after by the city, is probably worth a great deal more than the Eminent domain - the advantage of the Sovereign over the Vassal.

The *60 Minutes* program also pointed out another example of condemnation via the "blighted" rational. In New York City, an area was characterized as blighted and the Court upheld the taking. The new owners emerged: *The New York Times*.

60 Minutes pointed out that the blighted approach failed in Mesa, Arizona, where the Court apparently viewed it as an unwarranted extension of the condemnation concept.

Homeowners may believe the home is indeed a castle, but consider the fact houses may become the target of a revenue-hungry city government when there is a chance of investors and increased revenue. Think it couldn't happen to you or your neighbors?

In Glendale, California, a 2004 redevelopment proposal was termed "a legal rip-off" by Professor Ralph Shaffer of Cal Poly-Pomona in a perceptive *Los Angeles Times* piece. He noted similar problems in the cities of Irwindale, Buena Park, Fullerton, and La Mirada.

My own City of Diamond Bar has wrestled with proposed redevelopment issues and the element of "blight."

CASE EVALUATION

Description by California Court of Appeal, 4-27-00: "Diamond Bar, composed of rolling hills and valleys, is located at the junction of two major Southern California freeways (I-57, I-60) in southeastern Los Angeles County. It developed mainly as individual and unrelated single family residential tracts, with a minimal amount of commercial and other related uses.

"Diamond Bar is an affluent suburban community with a median income of about $66,000 per year, average home prices exceeding $300,000, and a relatively low crime rate. Non-residential uses, including schools and parklands, comprise about 20% if the city's land area. Commercial uses occupy a mere 2% of the city's land area and are located along Diamond Bar Boulevard and portions of Golden Springs Drive."

Progress of Events

4-18-1989 City of Diamond Bar Incorporated

9-25-1995 General Plan adopted. Included is the statement: "There is a need to encourage a variety of new or expanded commercial uses and other non-residential development as well as investigate other funding mechanisms, to help finance City services, infrastructure and amenities."

7-15-97 City adopts a Redevelopment Plan via Ordinance 3-97; 1,300 acres involved; physical and economic blight alleged; plan duration of 30 years' $405 millions tax increment expected.

8-1-97 Fifteen Plaintiffs file Petition for Write of Mandate to set aside adoption of Redevelopment Plan. (In a curious governmental ambivalence, 19 California cities filed an *amicus curiae* brief in support of the City of Diamond Bar; 7 California counties filed an amicus curiae brief supporting Plaintiffs.

1-11-99 Trial Court issues a Minute Order; "Writ of Mandate denied."

4-27-00 The Court of Appeal (Second Appellate District, Division Three) certifies for Publication is Conclusion: "We conclude there is no substantial evidence that the project area is blighted. Therefore, the judgment is reversed with directions to invalidate the plan.

The court of Appeal, in analyzing the plaintiffs "Fourteen Principal Cause of Action" allegations, emphasized several interesting factors:

BLIGHT: absence of factual evidence; only 8.8% of all buildings in project area of 1.300 acres require moderate or extensive rehabilitation, 73% of commercial buildings do not have vacancies.

PROJECT PURPOSE: the project has as its main purpose the capturing of a huge amount of tax increment for funding public improvements and recapture of city revenues lost through recent state legislative actions.

CONCLUSION: to invoke the extraordinary power of community redevelopment. It is not sufficient to issue a report and to adopt an ordinance speaking in the statutory language. The purpose of the Community Redevelopment Law (CRL) is to provide a means of remedying blight where it exists. The CRL is not simply a vehicle for cash-strapped municipalities to finance community improvements.

ADDENDUM TO CONCLUSION: We recognize the statutory definition of blight has evolved over the years. However, as stated just two years ago in County of Riverside, 65 Cal. App. 4th at pp 627-628, "true blight" is expressed by the kind of dire inner-city slum conditions defined in the Bunker Hill case; unacceptable living conditions of 85%; unacceptable building conditions of 76%; crime rate of nine times the city's average, and the cost of city services more than seven times the cost of tax revenues.

Another case in which blight was exemplified is Morgan vs. community Redevelopment agency (1991) 231 Cal App. 3d 243. Blighted conditions in Morgan included: unacceptable building conditions of 63% including 25% seismically unsafe commercial buildings; transient rentals; high crime rate; large homeless and runaway population; depreciating property values; an no likelihood of private development and investment.

The Court of Appeal's clear, supportive and decisive action in reversing the trial Court's judgment does not reflect one disturbing aspect of Diamond Bar's efforts to take over 1,300 acres of the communities land under the umbrella of California's community redevelopment law. That disturbing aspect is described only in the plaintiff's "complaint to determine validity of redevelopment plans and proceedings, for declaratory and injunctive relief," and has to do with city government's relationship with its citizens.

Consider the report of council, the primary document which set forth the factual evidence supporting findings and determinations required by the California community redevelopment law to support and adopt a redevelopment project. It was not made available to the general public until May 20, 1997, according to the plaintiff's "twelfth cause of action. The plaintiffs emphasized May 20, 1997 was the date of the project and on that date the plaintiffs appeared at a public hearing. It commenced at 10:30 pm and ended 45 minutes later. A rigid 5-minute per-speaker limit was enforced and speakers who asked permission to present video tapes of the project area were refused that opportunity.

The Court of Appeal, in examining "contentions," added a footnote in which it described its reaction to the restriction forbidding the use of videotapes of the proposed project and, having viewed the plaintiff's videotapes in their entirety admitted not having perceived anything remotely resembling blight. The videotapes depicted modern, well maintained, retail and office structures, amidst ample landscaping and open space, in a partially rustic setting.

A significant lesson from the Diamond Bar case involved the fifteen residents who tried to talk with the official city representatives. Some of the fifteen were characterized as "gadfly types," as "protestor types," or "troublemakers." Certainly, they were not "popular."

Notwithstanding, it was the group of fifteen who went to court and defied a majority of the "let it alone" citizens. Those fifteen fought for their concepts. They brought about a court-mandated victory. Government representatives have special responsibilities; one of these is listening. Another is respecting their citizenry. What a blessing is our country! Our republic has room for dissidents, for protestors!

The problems posed by the several examples which introduced this chapter, the city of Lakewood, Ohio; New York City; and Mesa, Arizona – as well as the city of Diamond Bar, California, are problems exacerbated by the creation of an addendum to the condemnation process. The addendum of an invasive weapon called "blight" can be manipulated to destroy the concept of "home."

The English barons who forced King John to meet with them "at the meadow which is called Runnymede, between

Windsor and Staines" on June 15, 1215, did their job. They cut down extravagant abuses of power by the Sovereign. They defended free men and their properties. They demanded lawful judgment of peers within the law of the land.

Yet, today, the Sovereign may emerge and achieve singular attention and recognition by the government of the United States and Homeland Security. Just as the word blight (a portmanteau expression) can be crammed with many meanings, the word homeland may also become burdened with interpretations. Will the land be made secure? Will the home become increasingly insecure?

From early law practice experience with condemnation proceedings in Norfolk, Virginia, and from some 24 years in right-of-way negotiation and appraisal for the state of California's highway department, I accepted the premise that private property is subject to appropriation by condemnation when needed for public purposes. Those included such uses as right-of-ways for freeways, school sites, airports, and military bases.

It was apparent that government agencies had to proceed carefully and thoughtfully in acquiring properties. Negotiation with property owners had to be based upon realistic well-prepared appraisals. Offers to purchase had to be fully, fairly, and respectfully tendered. If negotiations failed then condemnation was a last resort.

Many affected property owners consider the expression "last resort" as the government's use of a condemnation bludgeon to force the conclusion of the transaction. Anger, to the point of community rage are characteristic of some of the acquisitions. I witnessed negotiations conducted by some bodies that added fuel to the rage, such as property owners not permitted to see the "approved appraisal" of the property. Such practices are often a cover for offering less money than the full amount contained in the official appraisal.

It was a particular pleasure for me to participate in the creation of a federal requirement that allowed all property owners facing condemnation on a federally-funded project to see the approved appraisal in order to be assured a fair market value settlement offer.

It is appropriate to conclude with a celebrated definition of market value issued by the Superior Court of Sacramento County, on February 14, 1906.

"The highest price," wrote the Court, "estimated in terms of money, which the land would bring if exposed for sale in the open market, with reasonable time allowed in which to find a purchaser, buying with knowledge of all of the uses and purposes to which it was adapted and for which it was capable."

For the market value definition to be involved in a condemnation proceeding, a multitude of things have to be involved, before and after. It is a kaleidoscopic complex of government-citizen relationships.

It is reminiscent of the scene depicted in Lewis Carroll's magnificently perceptive *Alice's Adventures in Wonderland* in which the King orders the jury to consider its verdict.

"Not yet, not yet," the Rabbit hastily interrupts. "There's a great deal to come before that!"

ADDENDUM

The U.S. Supreme Court, on September 17, 2004, agreed to consider the problems created by cities in condemning private properties in order to promote private business development, when it took on the case of Kelo vs. the city of New London, Connecticut.

The Institute for Justice noted that, between 1998 and 2000, over 10,000 instances in 41 states have been city initiated, condemning private properties for transfer to other parties who are private developers.

Thursday, June 28, 2005, the Supreme Court announced a 5-4 ruling in the Kelo case, holding that cities can seize the homes, businesses, or shops of unwilling sellers to promote economic development as long as the goal is to create new jobs or raise taxes. Such condemned properties need not be blighted.

An attorney from the Institute for Justice described the ruling as "a dark day for American homeowners," noting that "every home, small business, or church would produce more taxes as a shopping-center or office building."

According to the Court, that is good enough for eminent domain. Justice Stevens described, as a basis for the decision, the promotion of economic development as a traditional and long-accepted function of government. Furthermore, state agencies, city, and county boards deserve broad latitudes in determining what public needs justify the use of the taking process.

Justice Stevens was joined in the majority by Justices Kennedy, Souter, Ginsberg, and Breyer.

The decision directly affected the plaintiff and eight other New London homeowners. The city's plans to seize their properties via condemnation proceedings moved forward a plan to revitalize downtown with a new restaurant, hotel, marina, and office complex – all coordinated with drug company Pfizer Inc., with plans for an accompanying $300 million research center.

Dissenting Justice Sandra Day O'Connor noted that under the banner of economic development, "all private property is now vulnerable to be taken and transferred to another private owner."

Nothing would prevent the state from replacing a small motel with a Ritz-Carlton or any home with a shopping mall.

Justice Clarence Thomas wrote in the dissenting opinion that redevelopment plans most heavily bear on the poor, minorities, and the elderly.

"Over 97% of the individuals forcibly removed from their homes," he wrote, "were black."

It should be noted that California's law provides that cities may employ eminent domain for community redevelopment only in "blighted areas." Several other states, including Arkansas, Florida, Illinois, Kentucky, South Carolina, and Washington have created and enforced comparable restrictions on city redevelopment agencies.

In the eminent domain context, "home" is no longer your "castle." Hundreds of years of our celebrated common law inheritance have been legally trashed.

Our homes, our businesses, and our farms may be appropriated by a governmental entity seeking money. No property in America is safe.

All states should adopt legislation requiring redevelopment proposals to be based upon documented need to eradicate major, extensive community blight within the proposed improvement area. Additionally, states should expand the definition of "just compensation," – the payment of fair market value for the property appraised – to require additional payment for any added value which the property reflects, <u>after</u>, the taking, when considered as a part of the redevelopment.

Get accustomed to the reality: money and politics now transcend all American value systems. If your "home" is no longer safe from forced taking, think of the irony of our nation-wide Homeland Security system.

Perhaps your only recourse is your voice and your vote. It's not quite time for a "tea dumping" in the harbor.

Or is it?

19

Public Education

You can always count on America to do the right thing.
That is, after it's tried everything else."
—Winston Churchill.

Few writers have had more impact upon our Greco-Roman cultural inheritance than a Thracian slave associated with "the Seven Wise Men of Greece." That man is known as Aesop.

Aesop's fables have fascinated young and old for more that 2000 years. Remember what happened to the goose that laid a golden egg every day? Recall the dog in the manger? According to Aristotle, Aesop defended a politician who was on trial for embezzlement by reciting one of his challenging fables. Before he was put to death at Delphi about 564 BC, Aesop recited a fable during his hearing. Aristophanes called the fateful trial unjust and a murder.

Described as deformed and ugly, Aesop transcended his critics, compeers, and century. Perhaps the most stunning accolade ever received by a storyteller is the description by reformer and cleric Martin Luther. He considered the Aesop fables as "wisdom literature to be reckoned next to the Bible."

In our century, George H. Reavis has created a fable worthy of Aesop. His fable is clear, delightful, and relevant to our time. It is of inestimable value to all who hold education in great esteem and who are deeply concerned about the direction and perspective of public education.

To appreciate the significance of this new fable entitled "The Animal School," it is helpful to touch base with foundation strengths of our republic, to wit:

- Public Education
- Public Libraries
- Public Press
- Public Health

I treasure my copy of "The Animal School" because it relates to my concern that public education is floundering and moving slowly downward, seemingly trapped into "throwing more money at the problem." It appears to be weakened by the notion that increased intensity of standardization will produce unanimity of achievement which will satisfy the mantra "No Child Left Behind." The mantra is easy to embrace; it is warm, fuzzy, and conveys assurance of fair play conjoined with equality.

It does not bode well for the public education scene by noting that the U.S. budget has included as much as $27 billion to support the No Child Left Behind program. It does not bolster the status of our great public education system by witnessing the forced emphasis on English and math while Art, music, and social studies become of secondary import.

"The Animal School" fable is priceless because it identifies the basic issue of curriculum structure, illustrates the innate myriad differences between students, and the ineffectiveness of enforcing measurement mandates which disregard individual abilities or differences.

Author Reavis created "The Animal School" in the 1940s as a putative public school challenge via the public school bulletin.

The fable – in 237 words – from "Once upon a time" to "Does this fable have a moral?" is beautifully illustrated by Joyce Orchard Garamelle, with foreword and epilogue by Char Forstern, Jim Grant, and Irv Richardson. The work is simple: a small group of animals envision and create a school. The mandatory curriculum is specific: running, climbing, swimming, and flying.

The *dramatis personae*: Duck, Rabbit, Squirrel, and Eagle.

In the testing process, Duck excels in swimming but does not do so well running and flying. Rabbit is the star runner, but struggles in swimming. Squirrel is the top climber until he suffers a charley horse. Eagle proves troublesome; he refuses to climb a tree, but insists on flying to the top instead.

Surprisingly, other animals emerge in the class. An abnormal eel becomes valedictorian! Ubiquitous Owl, who follows the process as an observer, appears frustrated at the confusion and conclusion when he is asked the ultimate question: "Does this fable have a moral?"

When I hear that school is a business and test scores are the product, that students are mere widgets on an assembly line, that every child will be prepared for a college career, that the curriculum is driven by the tests, that we are teaching to the test, that curriculum standards and tests sound good on paper, call to "Get those test scores up!" and statements that allude "That's why even some teachers are cheating" – I turn to "The Animal School."

When I read that the U.S. Department of Education has taken a first-time show on the road in the No Child Left Behind Act, that critics dismiss the seven-city tour as a token gesture, that critics fault the law for being too rigid, underfunded and test oriented, that criticism of the act from teacher-oriented unions claims unattainable standards and forces teachers to focus excessively on standardized test preparation – I turn to "The Animal School."

It is for its simplicity that I rely on "The Animal School" for directness and relevance. No Child Left Behind may be a wonderful mantra, but what of its substance?

Public education is a great venue for the discussion of equal opportunity for all. However, compare it with another great American venue – sports. Of course, the comparison does not involve similar experiences, similar goals, or similar perspectives, but that's the point!

America loves and revels in sports. With great enthusiasm, over 500 U.S. athletes joined some 10,000 other contestants, competing in 29 specific venues at the 2004 Olympic Games. We are proud of our athletes who made the cut, who had the qualities, and made the finals.

Mark well the grim, omnipresent shadow-partner of competitive athletics – performance-enhancing drugs. And mark well the grim, omnipresent shadow of cheating and plagiarism, which are endemic in our schools at student, teacher, and administrative levels. What does this problem reveal about the quality, value, and worth of the current amalgam of curriculum, tests, product, and systems?

Few advocates of U.S. education reform have contributed recommendations more specific, relevant, or massively researched psychologist Harold W. Stevenson, co-author with James W. Stigler of *Learning Gap: Why Our Schools Are Failing And What We Can Learn From Japanese and Chinese Education*. Stevenson produced, with Shin-Ying Lee, a classic film entitled *The Polished Stones: Mathematics Achievement Among Chinese and Japanese Elementary School Students*.

In his book, Stevenson pinpointed major deficiencies in the U.S. system of education such as weak academic standards, overburdened teachers, misguided cultural beliefs regarding parental responsibilities, and the importance of student participative efforts.

A former resident of Ann Arbor Michigan, Stevenson died in a Palo Alto, California hospital on July 7, 2005. Antonia Cortese, vice-president of the American Federation of Teachers, called Stevenson a pioneer in cross-culture comparisons who "looked at family attitudes and priorities, teacher training and methods."

"Quality is never an accident," wrote John Ruskin, "but is always the result of intelligent effort." Few persons outside the world of academia are aware of the serious nature and extent of cheating and plagiarism problems that swarm through classrooms at all levels.

In general, the devastating facts are that between 50% and 85% of students nationwide are cheating, according to survey after survey.

Organizations devoted to ethics concerns include:

- Center for the Advancement of Ethics and Character, Boston University
- Josephson Institute of Ethics, Marina del Rey, California
- Judicial Programs, University of Maryland
- Character Education Institute, San Antonio, Texas
- Center for Academic Integrity, Duke University

Academic Honor Codes have been established at:

- University of Virginia, Charlottesville, Virginia
- Hood College, Frederick, Maryland
- University of Maryland, College Park, Maryland
- University of Delaware, Dover Delaware
- University of Miami, Oxford, Ohio
- George Washington University, Washington D.C.
- Colgate University, Hamilton, New York
- University of California, Davis, California
- Princeton University, Princeton, New Jersey
- Rice University, Houston, Texas

Surveys regarding cheating examples are included in the *Who's Who among American High School Students.* In that study of

3100 top high school juniors and seniors, results indicated that 78% admitted to having cheated and 89% said they considered cheating to be common at their schools.

In an Emporia State University study, students were asked if they had cheated in high school and 76% responded "Yes."

There have been several primary commentaries on ethics and cheating, including:

- *Readers Digest* in the October 1995 issue, published "Cheating in Our Schools; A National Scandal" by Daniel R. Levine. This article is a brief but outstanding overview of nationwide cheating.

- *APS Monitor*, January 1996 issue; American Psychological Association; "Are Professors Turning a Blind Eye to Cheating?"

- "Research Paper: "Nipping Colleges; Cheating at its Worst"; George Roche; Hillsdale College, Hillsdale, Michigan.

- "Classroom Instruction on Integrity;" Chapman University, Orange, California. "A Tale of Ethics; the Positive and the Negative".

- Scholastic Perspective; three Examples that reveal the Ethics Nightmare:

- A west Los Angeles, California high school teacher commented after a majority of 51 advanced placement college-bound students admitted to frequent cheating, stating "If we stopped our students from cheating they would be at a competitive disadvantage."

A former St. Louis, Missouri, high school principal called cheating a "national scandal. The only way it can be defeated is for every school to confront it aggressively. A Diamond Bar, California letter to the editor published in the *San Gabriel Valley Tribune* claimed that school districts "cave-in to irresponsible demands of parents who are advocating dishonesty in their children."

Examples of major ethics scandals include that of the Big Ten Conference, which stripped the University of Minnesota of its 1997 men's basketball conference championship for an academic fraud scandal that cost the team five scholarships.

In Fairfield, Connecticut, a cheating scandal rocked the famous Stratford Elementary School, a U.S. Department of Education Blue Ribbon recipient for years. The exposure received national attention as "School's Shameful Secret."

Here are three action plans that would confront public school problems.

THE GALE-OSBORN FIVE PRINCIPLES

A perceptive and constructive recommendation that would strengthen and redirect America's current education system for public schools is that advocated by Margaret Gale, executive director of Duke University's American Association for Gifted Children, and Hugh Osborn, an educational consultant. Basically, they are concerned the current attempt to bring up the bottom third student group is counter productive because of emphasis on rote learning within a mechanical structure of specialized lessons and mechanical tests.

The Gale-Osborn recommendation for a turned-around, successful education process includes five common-sense principles: (1) engage students; promote involvement and interest through participative activities. (2) employ the power of information technology. Don't force drilling and testing on students; urge attention to the learning techniques developed in games learning systems, free of drilling and testing. (3) involve students in the world of libraries, museums, parks, and historical sites. (4) return to social learning and make the school a real community, rather than an age-segregated aberration. (5) use the free market. Internet learning can be made available to parent-child study as a new opportunity in practical "home learning."

REMOVE DEAD WEIGHT REGULATIONS

Instead of doing something more, do something less! The state of California has a 12-volume education code containing about 7,745 pages of regulations which dominate the system. These must be interpreted, implemented, and enforced via a State Board of Education and a Superintendent of Education. Additionally, California's 58 counties have offices of education managed by a superintendent with the assistance of a board of education. These 58 counties embrace 1,002 local school districts, operating under the aegis of a superintendent and a governing board.

The above-described pyramidal monster, with its inherent micromanagement and suffocating fiats, contributes to the nullification of innovation. The bureaucracy cannot exist without on unceasing stream of paperwork, a stream more demanding and more important than the inculcation of ethical criteria and the encouragement of integrity-oriented student comportment.

SEVEN STEPS TOWARD IMPROVEMENT

Several years ago, the president of the Los Angeles Board of Education spoke out with a plea to lift the education code dead weight from the school system. He summarized his commentary by recommending that the system fund lower class sizes, repair old school facilities, repeal current education codes, replace codes with a clear, simple statement of what is expected of the system and what is expected of the students, provide protection of student/employee rights, and create a statewide framework for accountability regarding schools and school districts.

Additionally, he recommended the reduction of the layers of political control and move governance from the state capitol back to local communities.

How can we solve the cheating and plagiarizing problem? The creation of a statewide ombuds system might begin to address a solution.

An ombuds office could be empowered to investigate and eliminate unethical practices at student, teacher, and administrative levels in the public school system.

What is an ombudsman? The concept originated in Sweden, where the word ombuds translates as agent. The ombudsman acts as a public advocate, impartially and expeditiously handling public grievances" First established by Sweden's legislature in 1809, the official chosen was to be a person of "legal ability and outstanding integrity," and would serve a four year term.

Ombuds offices have been formed in the United Kingdom, Germany, Israel, Denmark, Australia, New Zealand, Finland, Spain, The Netherlands, Provinces of Canada, and some U.S. States. Ombudspersons may currently represent businesses and industrial corporations; some U.S. college and universities have adopted the concept.

For the sake of case illustration, permit me to hypothesize that the state of California moved to adopt an ombuds office program authorized to investigate and confront, in an effort to diminish cheating in our public schools.

Where might the program start? The logical starting point would be the 107 community colleges, the workhorse of the 4-level State system and current "re-mediator" for K-12 students. They are the teaching processor for the great majority (70%) of the state's college-bound students; the world's largest system of higher education; educator of more than 1.4 million people a year. The system is community-based and oriented, and uniquely responsive and affordable for local citizenry.

It would be interesting to initiate the ombuds process at Mt. San Antonio Community College. In 1945, when the institution was created, ten Southern California cities formally adopted the proposed college's expressed philosophy that "No community of people will advance beyond the state of its educational system."

Thus, the proposed solution of creating a statewide professional ombuds system would have as its primary mission the investigation and confrontation of issues of cheating and plagiarism, to bring to a halt this pandemic academic disease.

This plan confronts the situation described in a 2000 Rutgers University survey wherein nearly 88% of the faculty "observed some form of serious cheating," and yet 32% did nothing. Professors feared legal liability that might arise from allegations of cheating, and worried that they would ultimately find themselves "sitting in the administration building with the parents and the family lawyer."

Is there any experience indicating a state ombudsperson can successfully cope with a vast system of fraud and sham? Will cheating, endured and sometimes encouraged by a populace indifferent to the academic nightmare in which students must compete, continue to exist?

In 2000, when Peru faced claims of rampant voter fraud, bureaucratic dishonesty, cheating, and trampling of civil rights, the legislature created a national ombudsman office. It was empowered to investigate, confront, and correct. Action was swift and the results were stunning. President Alberto Fujimori was forced out of office, his administrative corps removed, and the fraud and cheating was diminished. According to polls, ombudsman Jorge Santistevan and his office "received a higher approval rating than any institution in Peru except the Roman Catholic Church."

Action must be taken to confront the ethics crisis and cheating in public schools. In the January 1996 issue of the American Psychological Association *Monitor,* Patricia Keith-Spiegel and Lisa Gray-Shelberg were quoted as citing academic dishonesty as "one of the most serious problems facing higher education today." The two portrayed professors as being "anxiety ridden" about the issue, a condition they claimed as one that would reduce the validity of a student's education.

Shakespeare spoke to the heart of the matter: "No legacy is so rich as honesty,"

20

Sculptures

*In the millennial procession, humanity's monumental
historical sculptures emerge in an all-life-saving three-story
wooden Ark; the ponderous megaliths of Stonehenge; the
pyramidal glory of Egypt (the lone survivor of the Seven
Ancient Wonders of the World); a monstrous Trojan
Horse; the 500' Pharos of Alexandria; the Colossus of
Rhodes; a 120' bronze statue of the Sun God Helius;
Olympia's 40' statue of Zeus; the Sleeping Buddha in
Afghanistan; Peru's 2,400 year old astronomical device
the Thirteen Towers of Chankille serving ancestors of the
Inca.*

Sculptural symbols are intertwined with myths, fable,
parables – and facts – that reflect the aspirations and
creativity of many cultures. Such is Homer's fable of the
tragic fate of Laocoön and his sons who were strangled by
two monstrous serpents of the sea. Laocoön, the priest of
Neptune, attempted to save the city of Troy from the
duplicity represented by the Trojan Horse, or as Virgil wrote

it – *Timeo Dancaos et done ferentes* – "I fear the Greeks, even when they offer gifts."

The statue of Laocoön and his sons is one of the most celebrated groups of statues in existence. The original work was crafted by three artists from the Rhodes School of Sculpture, and is located in the Vatican.

Another fable involved Icarus, the youth who covered himself with feathers, string, and wax, to fly up and away but strayed to close to the sun. The wax melted and he fell into the sea and drowned. His father buried Icarus in the land called Icaria.

It is – all – the other wonderland of humankind that is, commemorated and preserved by monumental sculptures, megaliths, chards, bones, fiber crafts, feathers, metals, and shells, together with myths and fables. Think of the story about flood waters

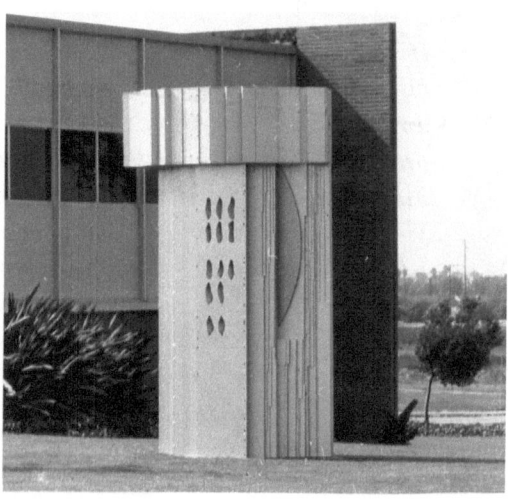

MU 464: CA State College, Long Beach 1964

upon the earth, "to destroy all flesh," in which the great deep is broken up "and the windows of Heaven opened." Remember the enormous wooden structure constructed to survive the deluge and save all life, an ark 450' long, 75' wide, and 45' high, covered with pitch. It was to be a three-story structure with a window and a door, but no rudder for steering and designed only to float aimlessly!

Give a thought to Noah, the reluctant amateur, versus the technological experts who built the Titanic! Consider further the rudderless ark.

Two of our major concerns today have to do with "govern" and "government." These words, of Latin origin, mean "to steer" or "to guide." Noah's Ark, a floating, rudderless wooden creation, is the first recorded sculptural argument for "no steering", "no government!"

From the vast reaches of the Pacific, noted for the immense enigmatic figures of Easter Island (Rapa Nui), to the mystery of the megaliths of Stonehenge and superseded archaeologically by few other than the stone circles in the Sahara, megaliths are powerful remnants of long-ago cultures.

Small stones (Greek = *lithos*) have also exerted powerful influence upon cultures, such as the stone tablets of Mt. Sinai, the Kaaba Stone in Mecca; and the Rosetta Stone in Egypt.

It is not my intention to imply indifference to the Western hemisphere's multitude of contributions to sculptured

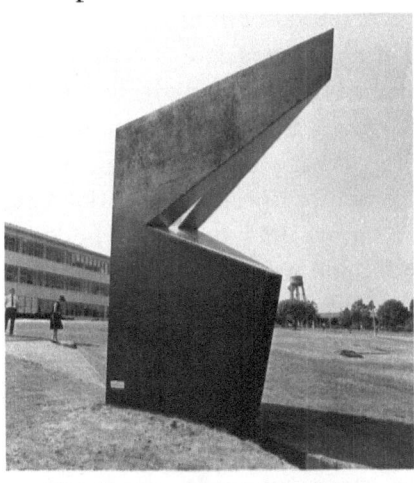

monuments. Artists from our hemisphere have produced magnificent sculptures and monolithic structures, including the massive Olmec Heads of basalt, the Toltec-Aztec giant pyramids of the sun and moon, the beautiful city-temple structures at Copan, Mitla, Monte Alban, Chichen-Itza, Bonanpok, Tikal, and Palengue, along with the totemic symbols of tribes.

Hardfact by Kosso Elool 1964

However, it must be emphasized that Western hemisphere cultures present considerable difficulty when trying to describe and understand their histories in terms of scientific fact and fable documentation. In general, four great societies dominated the hemisphere: Mexican, Mayan, Andean, and Yucatecan, Sculptured artifacts, together with massive stone ruins and remains of roadways and irrigation systems, provide principal sources of information adumbrating these cultures.

This is especially true in North America, in the area we know as the United States. For example, around 1500 BC, a people known as the Adena created spectacular mound earthworks in the Mississippi River basin. The Great Bird Mound in northeastern Louisiana was 70' high and had a wing span of 640'. The Great Serpent Mound was 1200' long.

A unique archaeological site on Florida's Atlantic Coast near Cape Canaveral is the early middle archaic Windover Bog, a pond cemetery for hunter-gatherers between 8120-6990 years ago! It has produced 87 samples of weaving, basketry, wood works, and clothing, as well as two treasures of middle archaic perishable artifacts!

Notwithstanding our quick review of a few of the monumental megalithic structures documenting early cultures worldwide, we must recognize and appreciate the power of the myths, parables and fables associated with them. An outstanding example is the Tower of Babel. It was thought to have been a gigantic Ziggurat, perhaps six stories in height, built to "reach heaven.' That structure is said to have become, at once, a flash-point impacting world language. The one-language world was split asunder and many languages arose as a punishment for the Babylonian builders and their audacity in creating a structure to reach heaven.

Communication was to be confused forever!

Present day sculpture in its broadest context and purpose includes the art of creating, building, carving, and forming symbolic figures and structures. It is centered upon a narrow niche in time, the 20th and 21st centuries in the United States.

Despite the limited time niche, a brief review regarding early U.S. monumental structures is relevant. One is the Washington Monument, a 555' high white marble obelisk with window openings at the 500' level. Another is the Statue of Liberty, 305' high, and the work of French sculptor Auguste Bartholdi.

Both magnificent monuments were undertaken in the 1800s. Few realize that Bartholdi designed around 1860, a great sculpture to be called "Egypt Carrying the Light." It was intended to serve as a lighthouse at the Suez Canal. The model he created was a virtual *maquette* for the eventual 305' sculpture of Liberty to be used as a gift to the people of the United States. (Many sculptures arise from initial *maquettes* or small models preceding the later proposed major final product.) My own modest effort – an eight-foot wooden sculpture created to honor Leonardo Fibonacci (1180-1250) was preceded by a 6" *maquette*.

In 1935, the Jefferson Memorial National Park was established in St. Louis. The Gateway Arch is coruscant, magnificent. Its dimensions are staggering: at 630' high, it is the tallest man-made monument in the Western hemisphere and is 75' taller than the Washington Monument and 180' higher than Egypt's Great Pyramid.

1954 witnessed the completion of a 35-year one-man project in Los Angeles, California. It was described in a resolution issued by the International Association for Art Critics as a structure representing a "unique combination of sculpture and architecture and a paramount achievement of twentieth century folk art in the United States." In the Watts Towers, steel rods are enveloped in mortar and discarded materials are used as ornamentation. The spiraling towers have brought forth enthusiastic reviews such as that of author Barbara Jones, who wrote in *Follies and Grottos* that the cones of spirals are beautiful and on a gigantic scale "for one man's work [and] superior to all but the finest work of the eighteenth century."

Located on a triangular piece of property adjacent to railroad tracks, the very conspicuous towers angered some neighbors in the Watts community. So intense was the

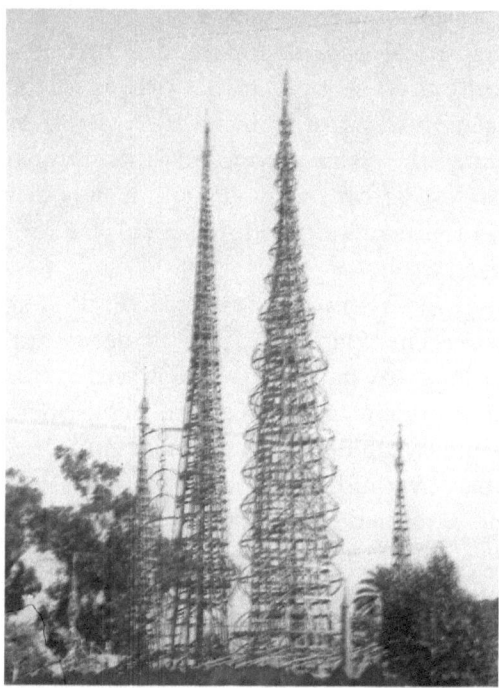

Watts Towers, Los Angeles

opposition that it was alleged the 100' high Towers were unsafe in the event of an earthquake. After years of contention, Los Angeles officials issued an order "to remove the dangerous towers." The order was ignored by builder and sculptor Simon Rodia. Eventually, the department proposed a test of one of the tallest towers to determine its safety. In October 1959, rigging and heavy equipment were attached and stress gauges were readied. The "pros" and "cons" (those who wanted the towers to be preserved and those against) crowded the area. Cameras focused on the unique challenge as the stress test began. Machinery growled and the structure withstood the pressure! Shouts of joy came from supporters as only a single decorative sea shell dropped of the estimated 70,000 that were embedded in the structure as ornamentation.

The Watts Towers preservation triumphed. The structures remain today as testimony to the engineering skill of a man who created his life's dream in a fantasy sculpture of steel and mortar.

One of the most significant events in the world of sculpture was initiated by UNESCO, the United Nations Educational, Scientific, and Cultural Organization.

Participants in a series of "Sculpture Symposia," – of which some 18 have been held since 1959, including 5 in Austria; 2 in Berlin; 7 in Yugoslavia; and 1 each in Tokyo, Spoleto, Israel, and Montreal – were invited to Royaumont, France, to form the International Sculpture Federation.

Kenneth Glenn, a professor of sculpture at California State College, Long Beach, attended the Royaumont meeting as the U.S. delegate vested with responsibility to organize the first International Sculpture Symposium in the United States.

Upon his return, Glenn contacted leaders of sculpture in Italy, Austria, Israel, Canada, and Yugoslavia. As a result of the cultural exchange, a monumental program was achieved. Objectives were outlined, including materials and techniques, and the groundwork was established for the first symposium in the U.S.

With Glenn's guidance, California State College, Long Beach became the first site of the U.S. Symposium in 1965. Some of the world's outstanding sculptors agreed to serve as instructors.

The total California arts community endorsed the idea, including the California Arts Commission, the Community Board of Supervisors, the City of Long Beach, and the art museums of Los Angeles, Santa Barbara, Pasadena, La Jolla, and Long Beach.

The budget amounted to $90,000 and Cal State Long Beach contributed about one third. The remainder was raised by Southern California art lovers. Forty industrial firms agreed to supply materials, services, and consultations.

The college included the event within its regular sessions. Each of the student instructor-sculptors agreed to produce a monumental structure with his or her students. The artworks would remain on permanent exhibition on the college campus. A modest stipend was provided each instructor, and the symposium supplied travel expenses, food, and lodging for eight weeks.

Artists exhibiting at the Symposium

- Kengiro Azuma – born in Japan in 1926. Works in bronze, steel.
- J.J, Beljon – born in Holland in 1922. Director, Royal Academy of Fine Arts, The Hague.
- Andre Bloc – born in Algiers in 1896. Created "sculpture habitable"
- Kosso Eloul – born in Russia in 1920. Created "Eternal Flame" for national Memorial, Jerusalem.
- Claire Falkenstein – born in Oregon. As a California artist developed metal/glass sculpture techniques.
- Gabriel Kohn – born in U.S. Winner, Int'l Competition, for monument "The Unknown Political Prisoner."
- Piotor Kowalski – born in Poland in 1927. Noted for work in concrete and translucent polyester.
- Rita Letendre – born in Quebec, Canada. Muralist.
- Robert Murray – born in Canada in 1936. Works exclusively in metal.

Huge sculptures and a mural that explodes with color remain on the Cal State, Long Beach campus as a reminder of the First International Sculptural Symposium held in the United States. Stories carried in the news media appeared in the Southern California press, and in *Life, Sunset, House and Garden*, and *Art d'Audourd'hui* magazines, the *New York Times*, as well as a documentary produced by NBC.

It was a bold revelatory plan to conduct two weeks of sculpture classes outdoors on a public college campus, and open for all to see. They were splendid, imaginative works-in-progress. A cynosure for eyes throughout the world, the

Symposium produced enquiries from many countries and immediately encouraged initiation of similar symposia in Mexico City, San Francisco, Bangkok, Japan, and Holland.

The massive megaliths that remind us of Stonehenge, the Redwood that soars, the metallic definition of dynamite, and the student memorial to Simon Rodia, all speak to those who see, who understand, appreciate, and quietly rejoice.

Public Art Works in the City of Brea California

As a city with a population of about 35,000, Brea's citizens pledged in 1975 to institute a program of art in public places. The stated purpose was to intertwine "public art with the city's private growth and development."

The program has been astonishingly successful. In addition to the Performing Arts Theater and a nationally recognized art gallery, the outdoor art collection numbers some 141 sculptures. The well-recognized "percent for art" formula for city art programs has earned for Brea a reputation for premier cultural venues.

The partnership between city government, citizens, artists, and businesses, is a tribute to the community's vision and determination. With sculpture at every bend of the road, the entire city has become an outdoor art gallery. While the hyperbole is understandable, it is also descriptive of the many sculpture installations.

Not all communities are as fortunate as Brea. In dismal contradistinction, consider Arlington, Texas, which in 1986 celebrated the completion of the sculpture series, entitled Caelum Moor, by artist Norman Hines. It is considered the largest environmental art of its kind in the Western hemisphere. It appeared to be doomed to dismemberment and removal due to opposition.

The gigantic work, located on five acres north of I-10 freeway in south Arlington, was welcomed and celebrated upon its formal opening. Some 570 tons of massive stone slabs, a few 35' high, had been sculpted and arranged in five groups. These megaliths resembled in size and configuration, the famed Stonehenge.

The contemporary artist-sculptor, Norm Hines, was a professor of Fine Arts at Pomona College in Claremont, California. He worked on the pink granite megaliths (the same stone used for the Texas State Capitol) in a quarry near Marble Falls, Texas, and created a total of 22 pieces for placement at Caelum Moor (Caelum = "sculptor's tool" + Moor = a reference to England's swamp-like coastal lands).

Following the 1986 Caelum Moor completion, people picnicked in the stones' shadows, marriages were held there, and children played throughout the park. Sculptor Hines intended the place as one "where people could come and meditate, wander around and interact even if they don't understand what it means."

All went well for the acclaimed sculpture-park. Valued at perhaps $1.5 million, it was to be the centerpiece of a surrounding commercial development proposal.

Unexpectedly, ominous signs emerged. Talk arose of pagan ceremonies held at the megaliths. A letter sent by 20 community ministers claimed a "witchcraft encyclopedia" indicated that Stonehenge (similar in composition to Caelum Moor) was a known gathering place for druids, pagans, and witches. One minister told the city council that she had seen white-robed figures participating in rituals.

Caelum Moor was designed to be the artistic magnet of a 340-acre commercial development which included a lake and an amphitheater, all dedicated to the citizens of Arlington and The Highlands. The Park was built for about $3 million in 1985 by a development corporation. Abruptly, in 1989, bankruptcy and liquidation of the enterprise followed.

City officials faced both "the Stonehenge witch thing" and the bankruptcy proceedings. The result? Fortunately for the city, a new proposal for creating a mega-shopping center was available and the prospect of public contention regarding morality and religious issues could be avoided. The land occupied by Caelum Moor sculptures and park appurtenances became prime development property. The megaliths of Caelum Moor Park were removed and stored in a municipal warehouse. Progress (higher revenues, more shopping sales) took its place.

In October of 2009, the massive sculpture was rededicated after its restoration at a site near the Dallas Cowboys stadium near the Dallas, Texas suburb of Arlington.

The Federation Interstate and Defense Highway System

In 1975, I was privileged to participate in a national seminar held in Washington D.C., on the nation's highways environment, sponsored by the U.S. Department of Transportation, Federal Highway Administration.

Convinced the nationwide interstate highway system (Congress passed the $33.5 billion road-building program in 195 as the largest public works project in U.S. history) had many aspects which symbolized our culture, I urged recognition of the major components of the vast 41,000 mile complex of freeways: "bigness" (quantitative colossalism), mass, time, motion. Our roadways and interchanges have captured these concepts, and they are put to use all day and all night, year-after-year.

During the years that gigantic system was being created, I urged consideration of the need for a "roadside aesthetic program," that is, breaking monotonous segments of long roadway tangents with sculptures, especially pinpointing "transition areas" of off-ramps servicing nearby communities. They could serve as measures to prevent driving monotony and auto-hypnosis. All of these issues received scant attention. Indeed, even arguing for the planting of bushes, vines, and trees on roadway slopes was unsuccessful, except in cases of erosion prevention and control.

Finally, I put the public sculpture issue aside for years. In 1998, sculptor Norm Hines and I agreed to present "Public Art: Megaliths and Colossal Structures" before the student body at Mt. San Antonio Community College in Walnut,

California. The forum was ideal because of the college's national reputation and the fact that the campus of this educational leader did not contain a single outdoor sculpture!

It is hard to believe how far I missed the target in efforts to bring the subject of public sculptures and megaliths into the arena of serious consideration!

It was during the presentation that the truth occurred to me. There was no need to plead for mammoth sculptures! They already exist throughout California and many parts of the U.S. We see them whenever we travel the interstate highways, when we use the monstrous three-and-four-level interchanges, and when we use on-and-off ramps. These great concrete sculptures are open, visible, and useable day and night. We move through these huge sculptures. They are vital for transport, for motorized interaction.

Unlike museum displays open specific hours, often requiring payment for entry, the public owns their highways and their sculpted intersections. Even more, the highway sculptures represent our penchant for speed, for pragmatic use, and convenience. They reflect the concepts of mass, time, motion, and utilitarianism.

I worked in the Los Angeles office of District VII, Division of Highways. I knew and respected Marilyn Reece, the state's first licensed female engineer who led the design team of the San Diego-Santa Monica freeway interchange that opened in 1964. It was the first interchange designed in California by a woman engineer.

Little did I know Marilyn Reece would become recognized as the concept creator of one of the most beautiful and colossal highway sculptures in the United States!

1964 MASTERPIECE---CALIFORNIA DESIGN

The I-410 San Diego and I-10 Santa Monica Interchange

- *30 designs considered*
- *3 levels—30 lanes*
- *10 lanes for connector rds*
- *600 property parcels*
- *90 acres of R/W*

2,000,000 cu yds fill material
16,000,000 lbs reinforcing steel
81,000 ft, storm drain pipe
$10,000,000 R/W parcels
$25,000,000---total project

Design Features

- *Eight 2-land connectors, some 60 feet above ground*
- *Minimum design speed....50 mph*
- *Pre-stressed post tension bridges*
- *85 ft deep pilings*

MEMORIAL

Marilyn Jorgenson Reese

As the first woman in California to be registered as a civil engineer and designer of the San Diego-Santa Monica Interchange, Marilyn Jorgenson Reese was the recipient of the Governor's Design Excellence Award." Marilyn was admired and respected by her professional compeers at the Las Angeles Division of Highways. She died May 14, 2004. All of us – friends, team members, and highway employees – miss her. She has left high goals realized.

21

Arcosanti

A giant with the same proportion as an ordinary man would need to be made of far stronger material to be as strong; an inordinate increase in height would cause him to fall and be crushed under his own weight."
—Galileo.

If limits of scale are overrun, either a new level is reached or the old level collapses."
—Gyorgy Kepes

In Roman mythology, the Lares and Penates were minor household gods concerned with family matters. In a somewhat similar manner I suppose, children through the ages have created role models, whom they imagine as super, wonderful beings.

As a youngster, I imagined such models. Relevant to any commentary about life on the Water Planet: one of my models was Matthew Fontaine Maury, "Pathfinder of the Seas". My high school was named for the man who suffered a permanent personal injury causing a classification of "unfitted for active service" in the U.S. Navy. Notwithstanding, his skills were so important he was placed in charge of naval charts and instruments. He understood the oceans, the tides, and the currents. He charted these wonders and produced oceanographic data of incalculable value for shipping lanes. Oceanography became an important science. Later, Jacques Ives Cousteau was added to my hero roll. Cousteau, co-inventor of the aqualung, was an explorer of underwater worlds.

There were other models, of course. There was Sequoyah (Siqway), Indian genius and creator of a complex alphabetic syllabary consisting of 88 characters for the Cherokee Nation. Another model was Davey Crockett, (frontiersman, congressman; killed at the Alamo in Texas) who cast the sole vote against the abrogation of the United States-Cherokee Nation Treaty, which led to the tragic "Trail of Tears." It was an act that characterized the brutal forced-removals to the west of many eastern Indian tribes.

I am convinced that another addition to my pantheon of models should include that of urban planner, architect, philosopher, artist Paoli Soleri. An advocate of the concept captured in the word arcology (architecture and ecology encompassed as one integrated process), Soleri has designed, and is creating, a venture in living creativity within an arid land, in a small, unique, specially-sculpted, and aesthetically designed community. The venture, is a community called Arcosanti.

Newsweek magazine described it as "probably the most important undertaking in our lifetime." Basic to the project: Arcosanti ties the praxis of qualitative minimalism to the securing of maximum benefits to the community members.

Soleri, in his 1993 book *Arcosanti: an Urban Laboratory,* includes a vision of life as "a wet phenomenon. Each living cell is a little sea of teeming events." He points out that nearly one-third of humanity is on arid land and that a chance exists for an "arid land culture" in the fashion of ancient examples.

Soleri's amazing experiment in the desert intends to develop new ways of thinking for achieving optimal city and community living.

EXPERIMENT IN THE DESERT

Aesop, in his telling of the fable of the frog, said that "a balloon made with certain elastic properties bursts when blown up beyond its limit." A city's traffic cannot be increased beyond a certain number of cars without defeating the purposes of speedy transportation. In metropolitan areas now, motor traffic has slowed down to the pace of horse and buggy days.

In 1965, Soleri created the new landscape Cosanti Foundation. For some forty years, building an experimental urban prototype has been the prime objective. In literature, workshops, and special programs it is emphasized Acrosanti is not a "city," but a demonstration model of creative concepts in urban design. As Soleri described the vision of mission and project, it is a "self-testing school for urban studies, a place where teaching and living will go on in an environment that is, in fact part of the lesson itself."

Arcology – the combination of architecture and ecology – is the driving concept, one capable in theory of demonstrating positive response to the many problems of urban civilization. Population, pollution, energy and natural resource depletion, food scarcity, and quality of life can all be addressed. Arcology recognizes reorganization of the urban landscape into dense, integrated, three-dimensional cities as possible.

Arcosanti is located 65 miles north of Phoenix, Arizona at Cordes Junction, Interstate 17, almost midway between Phoenix and Flagstaff. The 25-acre community-experimental core-space is embraced by a 4000 acre leased preserve on high desert mesa; it is a vast, arid land. The Hopi and Navajo Indian reservations are northeast of Arcosanti; the Haualapai

Indian reservations are southeasterly; and the O'Odham and Gila Indian reservations are to the south.

The ghost towns of Gleason, Paradise, Charleston, Harshaw, Mowry, and Ruby are on the U.S. side of the border with Mexico, along with the U.S. Fort Huachuca Military Reservation, four national wildlife refuges (Buenos Aires, Cabeza Prieta, Kofa, San Bernardino), and five national monuments (Chiricahua, Iron Forest, Sonoran Desert, Organ Pipe Cactus, and Casa Grande).

Arizona embraces some 114,000 square miles of a beautiful, immense wonderland and some 5.5 million persons. Surprisingly, only about 5% of the population is Native American. The Colorado Plateau in the northern area of Arizona, - the Grand Canyon State – is dominated by that incredibly beautiful canyon, the Colorado River, and Lake Mead. There is found the Grand Canyon Parashant National Monument and Park, and the Vermillion Cliffs National Monument. Indian Reservations in this area include the Havasupai and Kaibab.

Into the midst of these desert wonders, in the ancient lands of the indigenous people, Arcosanti has been introduced. It is a miniscule, experimental community intended to be a rejection of our current Anglo-European-American concept of the "modern city." In a strange way, perhaps only the Indian – the Hopi especially, whose pueblo dwellings on the High Mesas reflect recognition of and respect for complexity, miniaturization, and duration – can understand the pragmatic relationship and dependence upon the fecundity of arid lands.

Perhaps John E. Burchard (Dean, School of Humanities and Social Studies; M.I.T.) best expressed the concept in the foreword material of *The New Landscape in Art and Science* by Gyorgy Kepes.

"It has been the nature of our age," he wrote, "to place the word above the picture, the prose above the poetry, the problem above the tragedy, the search for truth by the methods of science above the search for truth by the intuitive methods of the artist."

When I visited Arcosanti in August 2000, I was interested in observing the project which Soleri saw as one in which "the planet is richly endowed" with so-called marginal lands. Far from the main transportation networks, hard to colonize, and poor in resources, such lands are for the most part beautiful and at times inspiring. These are reserves where future cultures might flourish, saving the fertile plains for much-needed crop cultivation.

In developing his theme, Soleri saw the experiment as part of a test to demonstrate community viability and self-reliance on such land, as well as an opportunity to explore the beauty and inspiration such environs engender.

Soleri saw the past and present as full of such occasions and insisted "from bacteria to God, three basic parameters are present: complexity, miniaturization, and duration."

The second major interest which impelled the visit to Arcosanti: I had just completed a brief study of another community in the town of Guadalupe, Arizona, an almost unbelievable, politically fortuitous, refuge for Yaqui Indians of northern Mexico. That group fled a genocidal government in Mexican government and resettled in Arizona.

It was my intention to compare, evaluate, and understand the two communities of Arcosanti and Guadalupe as they co-existed with their respective cities, large, centrally located, and modern.

A philosophic parenthetical: Phoenix (the axis), former territorial capital (1889) and current state capitol of Arizona, includes some 1,400,000 persons within its 475 square miles. It is very proud of its name *Phoenix*, a mythological bird of great beauty destined to live 500 years and then rise from the ashes of its funeral pyre and live again and again in wondrous immortality.

The Greek historian, Herodotus, claimed to have "not seen it myself, except in a picture." He described the plumage as "gold-colored, part crimson" and his appearance as "very much like an eagle in outline and bulk." Whatever the outline, whatever the bulk – what a magnificent symbol!

How curious it is that two unique communities – Arcosanti and Guadalupe – should have found their place near such an axis as Phoenix, determined to assert it can "rise from the ashes!"

Representatives of the Yaqui diaspora fled one homeland, found another, and are contributing to the preservation of old customs and creation of a new, present-day way of life.

Not far away from Guadalupe, Paoli Soleri is attempting to avoid the consequences that U.S.-established suburbs produce. He is attempting, rather, to create a new type of urban habitat. As he conceives the problem, it is one of municipal design, in which cities stretch outward for miles in unwieldy sprawl.

He sees the sprawl as contributing to the transformation of farms into parking lots, and to the time-wasting involved in moving people, goods and services. Soleri sees an alternative in "urban implosion, rather that explosion."

Guadalupe, refuge for the Yaqui is included in a U.S. city metroplex because of social and political compassion. Arcosanti, settled in high desert country in an arid environment, is dedicated to a future three-dimensional pedestrian environment with a possible ultimate population of 5000 people.

They are two unique and vastly significant communities facing the challenges of survival in a state with a great diversity of people, especially including inheritors of thousands of years of native culture. They are all hopeful for a safe, secure, productive future – all symbolically representative by a fabled Phoenix!

22

Wealth of Nations

Economy is in itself a source of great revenue.
  —Sepeca (4 BC- 6 AD 65)

If you know how to spend less than you get, you have the philosopher's stone.
  —Benjamin Franklin.

conomy, as a word is derived from the Greek words *eikos*, meaning "house" and *nemien* meaning "to manage." The Greek concept of economy was simply managing the house, or good housekeeping. Winston Churchill noted that "it saves a lot of trouble if, instead of having to earn money and save it, you can just go and borrow it."

Economics is the science that investigates conditions and laws affecting the production, distribution, and consumption of, or material means to satisfy affairs of household.

The term "political economy," or Blackstone's Public Economy, used in medieval and later times, in its literal sense denoted the art of managing the business affairs of a government, just as domestic economy denoted the art of managing the business affairs of a household.

Adam Smith was an author with a vision of society's great survival engine) and of the revolutionary environment of the 1600s and 1700s. Henry Thomas Buckle called Smith's *Wealth of Nations,* published in 1776, "probably the most important book which has ever been written." Harry Elmer Barnes allowed that it is "the great work of the leader of English Classical Economists."

The Wealth of Nations was recognized as a landmark of human thought even upon its publication in 1776, and the University of Chicago Press called it "the first successful argument for the principles of political economy."

The book is an enquiry into the nature and causes of the wealth of nations, and was published in the frenetic, revolutionary era experienced by England, France and the American colonies. It received world-wide attention and acclaim, and now appears in a fifth edition translated into eight languages.

According to author Smith, ten years were devoted to writing and production of his work. Such concepts as free enterprise, market place operation, supply and demand, and the invisible hand, earned for the magnificent opus recognition as the bible of economic theory. Today, the basic theories Smith propounded are respected throughout economic, business, political, and philosophical strata worldwide.

Adam Smith was born June 5, 1723 in Kirkcaldy, county Fife (about 10 miles north of Edinburgh, Scotland). Kirkcaldy was a small community of about 1,500 people, some of whom were at that time, using nails for money. It is said that when Smith was about 4 years old, he was kidnapped by gypsies, but was quickly rescued by an uncle who found the child abandoned on a country road. It was perhaps the most unique event in Smith's otherwise seemingly uneventful life.

At age 14, Smith attended the University of Glasgow, then moved to Oxford for six years, during which time, in apparent despair, he noted "the greater part of the public professors have, for these many years, given up altogether even the pretense of teaching."

About 1751, Smith became Professor of Logic, and later Professor of Moral Philosophy at Glasgow University. In 1759, he wrote "The Theory of Moral Sentiments" followed by a series of lectures on jurisprudence and literature. In the "Theory of Moral Sentiment," Smith wrote as a philosopher, not as an economic forecaster.

Smith never married, but lived in Edinburgh most of his life with his mother. It was from 1766 to 1776 that he was occupied with writing *Wealth of Nations*. It is reported he dictated the text while leaning against the fireplace at his home in Kirkcaldy. He described this period of his life as happy, energizing, and fulfilled.

In 1777, he served as commissioner of customs for Scotland. He died in Edinburgh on July 17, 1790.

For a man whose life has been described as remarkable only for its placidness, Smith created an explosive concept which moved center-stage into the revolutionary 1700s. It offered a new model for effectiveness in government and longevity in survival.

To understand the book and the man, you have to contemplate the environment of the time, especially in Scotland, in England, and in the American colonies.

In Scotland, the mother of twenty children might see only two survive. Child labor, malnutrition, disease and cold took a terrible toll. In England, one-half of all children died before age 4.

Despite – or because of - these conditions, a great wave of change was taking place, probably a major inheritance from the renaissance and the reformation. An age of discovery witnessed the emergence of the printing press, mechanical clocks, and paper mills, and all were symbols of an industrial revolution.

Old, cherished concepts were dying. In the middle ages, the church taught that "no Christian ought to be a merchant." In the American colonies in 1664, a well-known man was put on public trial in Boston for making a profit by charging interest. In France at about the same time, clothing manufacturers tried to trade for imported calico. The government punished the entrepreneurs, and seven were hung.

The longest, most labor intensive process was preferred. Advertising was forbidden. The conduct of a master guildsman trying to produce a better product was deemed treasonable. Guilds raised a hue and cry when tailors made cloth buttons and the government fined the button makers and those who wore them.

Despite the traditional environment of control, England was experiencing a golden age; Hobbs, Locke, Spinoza; Chippendale, Gainsborough, Defoe, Fielding, and Boswell. Mercantilism, conducted and controlled by the Crown and the merchant companies, was being challenged. In the American colonies, the Crown's imposition of taxes Revenue Act of 1764, included products such as silk, linen, sugar, wine, paint, lead, paper, and tea. The Stamp Act of 1765 covered licenses, pamphlets, newspapers, and almanacs. Both created deep resentment, especially – and surprisingly – regulations regarding tea. The ships Dartmouth, Eleanor, and Beaver arrived in Boston Harbor and people dressed as Indians boarded the vessels. Tea was dumped overboard. England responded with passage of the so-called "intolerable acts." Boston Harbor was closed and troops were dispatched. The British Parliament heard imprecations advocating "flogging everyone in Boston." A mandate prohibiting colonists from moving west across the Allegheny mountains added further burdens on the colonists.

In France the revolution was characterized in major part by two great, fervidly asserted slogans; *laissez faire* and *laissez passer* (literally, "let them do and let them pass). They summarized a doctrine that government should not interfere with commerce, and a parallel doctrine that a pass, especially one used in lieu of a passport should be allowed.

The waves of revolution generated new concepts, new perspectives, and a new understanding.

- Historically, "Trade" (despite land and sea routes never moved easily, safely, unencumbered among nations

- Creative ways of doing things was seldom a fundament of commerce and trade

- Making a living was seldom recognized as a means to an end concept; work was an inherited pathway of life

- The profit motive as a means of stimulating individual effort appeared as a very unusual concept

- The idea of land, labor, and capital interacting within a beneficial synergistic relationship was not realized until very recent times. The concept would have made very little sense in a pre-capital intensive market place.

Benjamin Franklin said the "use of money is all the advantage there is in having money." Survival of mankind until relatively recent times has been dominated by the environment. The search for food and shelter forced a focus upon the need for some type of group configuration and cooperation. The machines of cultures – the engines and governments that have energized tribes, fiefdoms, kingdoms, states, and nations, have taken two dominant forms, two engines, power sources for achieving and securing survival.

TRADITION assigns of tasks via custom. In ancient Egypt, every man was bound by a principle of religion to follow the occupation of his father. Consider the vast community of India, where social classes, privileges and occupations have been traditionally defined by caste.

COMMAND is the community controlled by fiat or by hortatory mandate. The central authority possesses the power to impose and enforce a behavioral system for all.

The two systems, tradition and command, have served as the great motivation and enforcement forces in history. Both have conducted wars; both have achieved the constructs of society's monuments. Leaders in religion, politics, the arts, philosophy, and the historian chronicling the events, functioned in one of the two dominating protecting environments. Mankind's masses have lived and died within one of the two great engines of society.

Because of complete domination by tradition and command engines, it may be assumed that is the reason there were few economists, as we understand the term and concept today. There was little need for economists in the traditional-oriented or command-propelled society. Few authors addressed the subject. Semantically, the Greek basis for the word economics identified management of a household and housekeeping little needed by philosophers and economists.

As brilliantly observed by Robert L. Heilbroner in *The Worldly Philosophers,* the problem – so long as it was handled by tradition or command – never gave rise to "that special field of study called economics." In summarizing the centuries-long absence of economists from the global scene of history, author Heilbroner concluded that there were theologians, political theorists, philosophers, and historians, but "strange as it may seem, economists, no."

In 1776, through the medium of Smith's ponderous masterpiece, the world's great survival engine appeared. I know of no more direct, competent descriptive summary of the event than that advanced by Heilbroner in his contention that "the travail was over and the market system had been born," and the problem of survival would be taken up by a new system that "was to be called capitalism."

Three of the most often quoted of Adam Smith's observations and conclusions:

> "It is not from the benevolence of the butcher, the brewer, or the baker, that we expect our dinner, but from the regard to their own interest. We address ourselves, not to their humanity, but to their self love, and never talk to them of our

own necessities but of their advantages."

"It is not for it's own sake that men desire money,   but for the sake of what they can purchase with it."

"The natural effort of every individual to better his own condition, when suffered to exert itself with freedom and security., is so powerful a principle, that it is alone, and without any assistance, not only capable of carrying on the society to wealth and prosperity, but of surmounting a hundred impertinent obstructions with which the folly of human laws too often encumbers its operations."

Regarding encumbering laws, Smith was clear and direct about government, and described three major responsibilities of the Sovereign or Commonwealth:

1. The first duty of the Sovereign, that of protecting the society from the violence and invasion of other independent countries, can be performed only by means of a military force."

2. The second duty of the sovereign, that of protecting, as far as possible, every member of that society from the injustice or oppression of every other member of it, or the duty of establishing an exact administration of justice."

3. The third and last duty of the sovereign or commonwealth is that of erecting and maintaining those public institutions and those public works... facilitating the commerce of the society, and those for promoting the instruction of the people."

LADIES AND GENTLEMEN, IT IS AN
HONOR TO PRESENT THE HONORABLE
ADAM   SMITH,   SCOTLAND'S
COMMISSIONER OF CUSTOMS: AUTHOR
OF THE WORLD FAMOUS, HIGHLY
ACCLAIMED BOOK, AN INQUIRY INTO
THE NATURE AND CAUSES OF THE
WEALTH OF NATIONS!

For years I have enjoyed the opportunity and
responsibility of responding to the introduction
characterizing my role as Scotland's Adam Smith;
commissioner, professor, lecturer and author of *An Inquiry
into the Nature and Causes of the Wealth of Nations*. I have
addressed social clubs, public school groups, conventions, as
well as corporate, business and professional assemblies,
dressed in a fashion reminiscent of the Adam Smith and
Benjamin Franklin era of the 1700s.

It has been a challenging experience. First, it took a while
to appreciate the significance of dressing the part, of
assuming the role. This lesson was demonstrated to me by a
truly talented man, Ralph Archibald of Philadelphia, PA., who
for years has been carefully, skillfully, and professionally
acting in the role of Ben Franklin as a full time career. He
lives the part. As he described his experience to me, he had
become Benjamin Franklin. As we talked over breakfast in a
small restaurant, I saw the interest of those around us, some
adults came and spoke to Ben, children were wide-eyed and
trusting, and came in fascination to listen to him. He was an
impressive, benevolent figure, a magnet of historical
significance from another time.

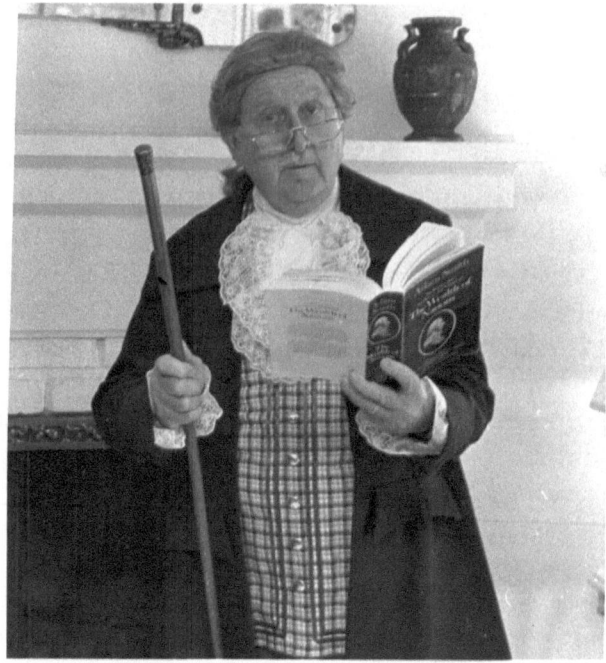

Dexter MacBride as Adam Smith

After breakfast, we drove through Philadelphia's streets. We came to a cemetery and he slowed, and then stopped. He looked over to the left, and then pointed and said, "I'm buried there."

We drove on in silence. I was stunned. He meant it! He had, I believe, assumed the persona of Franklin completely, devotedly, and sincerely. What an experience!

It has not been so all-encompassing a role for me in acting for perhaps 30 or 45 minutes during a presentation, but the dress up plays a strong part in delivering the message.

I hear myself, upon these public speaking engagements, saying important things, describing significant fundamentals in the words and terms I believe Adam Smith would employ. Clutching my copy of *Wealth of Nations* (568 pages worn and marked in dozen of sections; my book was published in 1976 by the University of Chicago Press), I might hear Adam Smith saying "The scope and process of the market place embraces a vast playing field in which all may participate and exercise a myriad of skills. Each player does what seems fit, for the best monetary advantage. This market place offers the powerful possibility of personal gain, as distinguished from tradition's belief adjurations, or Fiat dominate command results. All the players in the market place may choose their desired activity and anticipated goals; the resultant contention and competition promotes the productive and compensatory activities of society.

You must answer for yourself, the questions which will arise. Will the market system get the job done for society? If command and tradition are abandoned, will the vision of a great market place the concept of self directed participants creating a kind of invisible hand, produce the new survival engine for all societies, governments, communities of mankind?

23

Civil Disobedience ~ Satyagraha

Human history began with an act of disobedience.
—Erich Fromme

Human disobedience has indeed marked humankind's progress in matter of ancient religious concern. Illustrative instances include the banishment from the Garden of Eden, (Genesis 2,3); Babel Tower and the confusion of Languages (Genesis 11); the destruction of Sodom and Gomorrah (Genesis 18,19); Transformation of Lot's wife into salt (Genesis 19); and the exhaustive argumentation between God and Job (Job).

However, it is modern history that brings the issue of disobedience, specifically civil disobedience, to your attention. Civil is understood as consisting of citizens, the commonwealth or state; the ordinary life and affairs of citizens.

Wrestling with the issues and concerns presented by civil disobedience may be more relevantly traced using examples closer to our understanding and experience. Consider, therefore, the stunning example represented by the creation of the Magna Carta, celebrated for its impact upon our current civil law, and our Citizen's rights and liberties.

It was an incredible meeting in the meadow, one long anticipated, conceived, and debated. They achieved a majestic agreement, documented by the great contract, the Magna Carta. It was reached without the iron implacability of war. It is a testament to a specific consummation of agreement arising from the force of civil disobedience.

Sixty-three articles are included in the historic document. In the concluding words, the parties resolve that "the English Church shall be free, and that the subject of our realm shall have and hold all the aforesaid liberties, rights and concessions, duly and in peace, freely and quietly, fully and entirely, for themselves and their heirs."

There is a constellation of similar agreements, varying message, perspective, and purpose.

The Mayflower Compact of 1640 brought forth signatures of loyal subjects of King James of Great Britain, France and Ireland, convening and combining into a civil body politic to enact, constitute and frame just and equal laws, ordinances, acts, constitution, and offices.

The Declaration of Rights from the Congress at New York on October 19, 1765, and the Declaration of Rights from Congress at Philadelphia on October 14, 1774 are examples. The Declaration of Independence adopted by Congress on July 2 and signed on July 4, 1776 and the unanimous Declaration of the Thirteen United States of America are others.

The Articles of Confederation adopted in Congress July 9, 1778 with ratification formally announced to the public March 1, 1781, is also among the documents that were the stepping stones of civil disobedience, leading to the Preamble of the Constitution of the United States (convention of September 17, 1787) in which objectives "to form a more perfect union, establish justice, insure domestic tranquility, provide for the common defense, promote the general welfare and secure the blessing of liberty" are described in seven articles.

Fifty-nine delegates were chosen for the convention. 10 did not attend. 16 declined or failed to sign. Rhode Island sent no delegates. Four years later, on December 15, 1791, ten amendments to the constitution were ratified.

THOREAU'S CIVIL DISOBEDIENCE."

> *All men recognize the right of revolution; that is, the right to refuse allegiance to and to resist the government, when it's tyranny or its inefficiency are great and un-endurable....such was the case, they think in the revolution of '75"*
>
> —*Henry David Thoreau, in* Civil Disobedience

The lecture that was delivered at Massachusetts Concord Lyceum in February 1848 by a 31 year old author and naturalist Henry David Thoreau has captivated and motivated millions. Opening with "I heartily accept the motto that government is best which governs least," Thoreau also believed that "the government is best which governs not at all."

The lecture's concludes "is it not possible to take a step further toward recognizing and organizing the right of man? There will never be a really free and enlightened state, until the state comes to recognize the individual as a high and independent power, from which all its own power and activity are derived, and treat him accordingly."

"I please myself," wrote Thoreau, "with imagining a state at last which can afford to be just to all men and to treat the individual with respect as a neighbor."

Between these two mighty statements serving as prologue and epilogue appears four lines from Shakespeare:

I am too high born to be propertied,
To be secondary at control,
Or useful serving man and instrument,
To any sovereign state throughout the world.
   –King John.

Thoreau directed his lecture, principally at two issues of the time, the war between Mexico and the United States (1846 - 1848) and slavery. However, he reasoned and reached much further, speculating that "action from principle" and the perception of right "changes things and relations, and does not consist wholly with any thing that was. It not only divides states; aye, it divides the individual, separating the diabolical in him from the divine."

It is interesting to recall the often-quoted story about Thoreau's one night stay in the Concord jail for refusal to pay poll tax. He devoted 10 paragraphs in his lecture to the experience, but they do not contain the magical – albeit possibly apocryphal – exchange thought to have occurred between himself and Emerson.

Emerson: "Henry David, what are you doing in there?"
Thoreau: "Ralph Waldo, what are you doing out there?"

Thoreau's lecture closes with the iterated theme: "The progress from an absolute monarchy to a limited monarchy; from a limited monarchy to a democracy, is a progress toward a true respect for the individual. Is a democracy, such as we know it, the last improvement possible in government? Is it not possible to take a step further towards recognizing and organizing the right of man?"

The question Thoreau asked was answered about years later by India's Mohandas Gandhi, the leader who freed a quarter-billion people under the colonial tyranny of Great Britain. Gandhi read, understood, and cherished Thoreau's *Civil Disobedience* commentary.

SATYAGRAHA

"Non-violence has come among men and it will live. It is the harbinger of the peace of the world."
—M. Gandhi

Satyagraha is the word Gandhi employed to describe the process he used in confronting the British with a years-long program of active non-violent resistance, employed to free his country of two and a half centuries of British Imperial colonial control.

Satyagraha literally connotes, "true force" or soul force," power employed actively in non-violent resistance. Incredibly, Gandhi achieved the freedom he sought for a quarter of a billion of his people. India and Pakistan became independent dominions August 15, 1947. Burma became completely independent January 1948; Ceylon achieved dominion status February 1948.

Gandhi's struggle with the British reached its zenith and captured world wide attention because of the unbelievable "March to the Sea." The 200 mile trek began March 12, 1930. Gandhi and 78 men and women from his ashram (a religiously oriented community, often clustered around a holy man) started on foot to reach the Arabian Sea at the entrance to the Gulf of Cambay. It took 20 days over dirt roads and pathways winding through dozens of tiny villages and communities. As they marched, the villagers came to watch and marvel at the audacity of the participants publicly flaunting the law by marching to the sea to take salt which was against the strict provision of the British salt tax forbidding the practice to the Indian people. As the days passed in punishing heat, the procession drew thousands upon thousands.

The refusal to obey the government's ukase sent a message to India's millions which they understood, a message that smashed into British colonialism with a power they did not imagine or understand. Non-violence to governmental tyranny was being achieved through the focused energy of a leader completely dedicated to the power of Soul Force and Truth Force.

Gandhi received worldwide accolades for his inspired leadership. Albert Einstein's statement seemed to best summarize the vast symbolism of Gandhi's contribution to mankind and generations to come which "will scarce believe such a one as this even in flesh and blood walked upon this earth."

What was Gandhi's great contribution to mankind? Simply put: an alterative to war. He has given affirmation to the words of Jesus:

"Put up again thy sword into his place; for they who take the sword shall perish with the sword." (New Testament Matthew 26)

THE SLAVERY CONFRONTATION

In Mark 4:30 it is written:

"Whereunto shall we liken the kingdom of God, or with what comparison, shall we compare it? It is like a grain of mustard seed which, when it is sown in the earth, is less than all the seeds that be in the earth."

Whatever the comparison – a grain of mustard seed or the acorn presaging a giant oak – the pinpoint power to truth and soul force must be recognized.

It is my conviction that a single, signal, virtually unknown incident (certainly missing from the rubric of our modern history books) initiated and directed the most significant non-violent modern movement the world has witnessed prior to M. Gandhi's successful Satyagraha campaign which freed India in the 1940s.

The event occurred May 22, 1787 in a bookstore printing shop at 2 George Yard in London, England. Late that day, twelve men met and formed a committee to end the British slave trade and end the practice of slavery. James Phillips, proprietor of the shop, was printer for the British Quakers (members of the Society of Friends, colloquially called Quakers because the society's founder, George Fox, told them to "tremble at the word of the Lord").

It is necessary to recognize that the British were a major participant in the highly lucrative Atlantic African slave trade, shipping nearly half of all the slaves to the West Indies, the United States, and Europe.

The committee's book of minutes contains a one-page statement handwritten by Thomas Clarkson, the group's organizer.

"At a meeting," wrote Clarkson, "held for the purpose of taking the slave trade into consideration, it was resolved that the said trade was both impolitic and unjust."

Author Adam Hochschild, in his work *Bury the Chains: Prophets and Rebels in the Fight to Free and Empire's Slaves*, thoughtfully described the public's reaction to the resolution, pointing out that it was the first time many in a single country became outraged and stayed that way "over the plight of other people, of another color, in other parts of the world."

The small meeting of Quakers produced a resolution and a storm. Petitions flooded Parliament; debates, posters, and books sounded tocsins for the cause. Organizer Tom Clarkson traveled alone on horseback some 35,000 miles through England, Scotland and Wales during the group's early seven-year efforts.

The momentous energy and dynamism of these anti-slavery efforts were without parallel. Slavery abolitionists in Brittan and the U.S. had never received such massive support. Alex de Tocqueville, the brilliant French author and student of British and American government, wrote that the event was absolutely without precedent, and that even poring over the histories of all people "I doubt that you will find anything more extraordinary."

Without a doubt, author Adam Hochschild has discovered similarly, the essence, importance, and power of the George Yard event, the spirit that crystallized there is with us in a different way. In the idea that those who suffer no grievance or injury have the obligation to speak up for those who have suffered lies the birth of the vision that human rights are universal.

Who can doubt the power of the mustard seed, given the task, opportunity, and responsibility to employ that power for universal human rights?

Gandhi understood the power and force. He embraced, understood, and employed these forces to achieve an alternative to war, just as the 12 Quaker's understood and acted upon this understanding.

24

Mythology

The intelligible forms of ancient poets,
The fair humanities of old religion,
The power, the beauty and the majesty
That had their haunts in dale or piny mountain
Or forest, by slow stream or pebbly spring
Or chasms and watery depths: all these have vanish'd,
Coleridge (1771-1834)
     —Samuel Coleridge (1771-1834)

The human animal lives in many worlds;
Society, to escape itself, flees into the worlds of Myth, Fable, Folklore,
and Legend."
     —Anonymous

There are few persons who will deny the happiness brought to many children through the warm communicative medium of stories about Christmas, Santa Claus, reindeer Rudolph, Easter and its Bunny who brings colored eggs, the fairy with nighttime penchant for trading a reward for a tooth, or the assurance there really is a Great Pumpkin.

Adults in all eras have cherished fabulous visions in fables about the Fountain of Youth, of the Golden Cities of Cibola, of long-lost ships floating in the mists of the Sargasso Sea, of quests for the Holy Grail, and of a confrontation with some monstrous griffin or friendly unicorn.

In his classic work, *Mythology*, Thomas Bulfinch cites Samuel Coleridge's above description of the morning of life.

To the Greeks, the morning of life began on a flat, circular earth, divided by an east-west sea (the Mediterranean). Their flat earth was surrounded by a vast ocean. Mt. Olympus was perceived to be the home of the gods. Zeus, the father, was surrounded by many specially-gifted members of the majestic family, all of whom had emerged from Chaos. These included Hermes, Demeter, Dionysus; Satyrs; Nemesis; Pan; three Muses, three Graces, and three Fates.

The Fates, daughters of Themis (who was legal counsel for Jove) loom large in humankind's destiny. The three had an enormous responsibility. Clotho was the spinner of the threads of life. Lachesis measured the lifeline lengths while Atropos decided when to cut the threads.

Few have captured the magic of fables more effectively than Aesop, a Thracian slave who lived in the early part of the 6th century B.C. Associated with the "Seven Wise Men of Greece," and a Counselor to Kings, Aesop was murdered (presumably by one of the Wise Men) in 564 B.C. It is fascinating to note that Martin Luther, some twenty centuries later, considered Aesop's fables as "wisdom literature," to be reckoned next to the Bible. Among Aesop's fables, recall the two following examples of this magical insight:

The Dog in the Manger

A dog made his bed in a manger and lay snarling and growling to keep the horses from their feed.

"See?" said one of them. "What a miserable cur, who can neither eat corn himself, nor will allow those to eat it who can."

The Goose with the Golden Egg

A certain man had the good fortune to posses a goose that laid him a golden egg every day, but dissatisfied with so slow an income, and looking to seize the whole treasure at once, he killed the goose, and cutting her open, found her just what any other goose would be!

A prime example of a Greek legend is that of the story about Procrustes. He was considered to be a thug, a marauder, an evil doer, because of his attacks upon travelers. Procrustes, called "the Stretcher", would seize his victims and tie them to an iron bedstead. If the travelers were too short, he would stretch them until they fit; if too long, he would chop off the overhanging limbs. Fortunately for travelers, Thesus – the son of the King of Athens – attacked and killed the "the Stretcher."

Another legend is that of the great wooden horse which the Greeks constructed and left at the gates of Troy. The Trojans, weary of battle, thought the Greeks had finally abandoned the sedge and left the horse as a gift. The Trojans celebrated a presumed victory throughout the night. Then, when the Trojans finally slept, the Greek soldiers hidden inside the horse came out, opened the gates, entered the city, and put the bewildered Trojans to the sword.

A man called Laocoön pled with his fellow Trojans to be on guard and not drag the great horse in their city. His famous exhortation: "I fear the Greeks even when they offer gifts." (*Timeo Danaos et dona Ferentes.*) The gods, angry at Laocoön's audacity in interfering, sent two enormous serpents to the scene. The serpents attacked the priest and his two sons, enfolded the three in their coils and killed them. (Yes, the gods take sides in the Greek drama; they often reflected the churlishness and vindictiveness of humans.)

As author Thomas Bullfinch notes, "One of the most celebrated groups of statuary in existence is that of Laocoön and his children in the embrace of the serpents. The original is in the Vatican at Rome. The statuary is thought to have been created in the 2nd century B.C. Three artists in the Rhodes school of sculpture are presumed to have produced the magnificent work.

Roman Mythology

The people, the culture, and the society of Rome created concepts similar to the Greeks.

Concepts served as the nexus of humankind's other world. Like the Greeks, they envisioned many gods, Jupiter, Saturn, Bellona, Terminus, Pomona, Flora, Vesta, and Janus, to name a few. Smaller more intimate household gods were called Lares and Penates, important to families and involved in all matters related to activities, history and welfare.

A race of giants, the Titans, was represented Prometheus and his brother Epimetheus. The two were entrusted with providing all animate and mankind with proper equipment necessary in facing life. In so doing the also gave to man the supreme gift: the Magic of Fire.

The creation of Woman was achieved, by Jupiter's order. Pandora was the first woman. She was given by the gods to Epimetheus. Her possession of a gift box entrusted to her by the gods, led to disaster when she disobeyed the order to keep it closed. An array of plagues flew out. Only one force did not escape: Hope.

One of the great events of this mythic Roman world was the Iron Era, in which humankind centered attention upon weapons and warfare. So grievous were conditions that Jupiter decided to destroy all of earth's inhabitants; he would drown all the world and start anew. Rain, downpours and earthquakes, flooding rivers and lakes, and rising seas savaged the Earth. Mt. Parnassus was the lone mountain not completely covered. Jupiter saw two survivors in the water devastation, Deucalion and Pyrrha, a husband and wife noted for their faithful worship of the gods. Respecting their lives, Jupiter ordered the waters to subside. Neptune ordered

Triton to blow his wreathed seashell horn. The two survivors began rebuilding the new community of mankind.

The theater of Greek and Roman beliefs, concepts, and fears that dominated their everyday world of reality and survival contains interwoven myths filled with adventures of Ulysses and Cyclops. Circe and the Sirens. Scylla and Charybdis, Calypso and Aeneas. The island of Harpies. Queen Dido, the infernal Regions, the cave of Hell, and the ferryman Charon.

The three-headed Cerberus.

It is impossible to resist describing three inmates of Hell, led by Oxion, tied to the rim of an enormous wheel which turns, endlessly. The second is Sisyphus, the man who is forced to roll a great stone up a hilltop but just as it reaches the top, the stone slips and rolls back down. The third is Tantalus, standing forever in water up this his chin. When he tries to drink the water recedes. Over and over he tries, but he is forever parched. Tantalus, the son of Zeus, was condemned for revealing secrets of the gods. We remember him, semantically in the world *tantalize*.

Mythology preserves and perpetuates the idea of the need for an origin story of man's communities. The specific identification of a formal beginning creates a belief a strengthening resolution for proud full continuity. Romulus and Remus were two infants descended from Aeneas's son, who created Alba Loaga, which became the birthplace of the two beginners of Rome.

The Western Hemisphere

In like fashion, the Western hemisphere has legends in the founding of Tenochtitlan, now called Mexico City. Although it is incredibly difficult to identify, describe, and understand legends of pre-Columbian civilizations, native oral traditions about the Aztec's capitol survive. Codices and manuscripts composed of lime-coated bark were printed with a form of writing. These have communicated the story that the Aztec capitol was to be located in a vast lake (Lake Texcoco) area, on an island. The Aztec gods told believers the exact location would be recognized by a great eagle clutching a snake that would be perched on a cactus plant growing from the rock.

The people searched and found the spot just as it had been described.

So Tenochtitlan was formed, graced by the gods. When the marauding Spanish arrived, they were astonished at what they saw. Bernal Diaz, a soldier who participated in the Spanish invasion and occupation of Tenochtitlan, wrote that they were amazed at the number of cities and villages.

"It was like the enchanted things," he wrote, "because of the huge terraces, temples and building rising from the water and all of masonry."

An almost parallel mythological world existed throughout South America. Peru provides an interesting example in which the creation of the former great Incan capital city of Cuzco. The ancestors of the Incas, shepherds and farmers, lived on the high roof of the world. The Andes Mountains stand at an elevation of about 12,000 feet above sea level. The Inca sun god Inti created the people. Inti chose two children, whom he placed on an island, like Titicaca, and gave them a gold staff. He sent them forth to search for and find the spot for their people's central city.

The children searched and explored a beautiful sun drenched valley (The Sacred Valley of the Incas). When they plunged their gold staff into the ground, it disappeared. This was the sought-after place and the city of Cuzco was thus founded. (Cuzco is a derivative of *qusquo*, the Quechua word which means "navel of the world."

How powerful, how magnificent to be Center of the World.

<u>Parables</u>

Ancient stories are often double-edged, like a sword. Consider these two tales:

There was a time, long, long ago when the people of the Earth spoke but one language. The people decided they wanted to make a name and be recognized. They built a gigantic tower reaching toward the heavens. Their efforts brought them condemnation from on High. Their language was confounded the people separated and scattered abroad. This is the parable of Babylon and the consequent source of worldwide confusion of languages.

A similar parable concerns the earliest known city in the world. It is the story of Jericho, a fortress city besieged by an army of 40,000. It was a six day siege of the fortress, and on the seventh day, with trumpets sounding and fortress walls crumbling, the city was stormed, its residents burned except for one: a spy who helped the invaders.

The location? The West Bank, just north of the Dead Sea, close to the River Jordan.

And the warfare? It continues to this day over the same Middle East terrain.

<u>Popular Fairy Tales</u>

Danish author Hans Christian Anderson (1805-1875) produced many fairy tales. 29 are included in his book of wonder entitled *Anderson's Fairy Tales.*

The Emperor's New Clothes

Two swindlers, posing as weavers, claim to be able to produce the most beautiful clothes imaginable, cloth that had the peculiar property of becoming invisible to every person who was not fit for the office he held, or was impossibly dull.

The two put up looms and pretended to weave. As they

continued they demanded more money and more silk (which they pocketed). The Emperor paraded about in the new clothes, the onlookers saw nothing but exclaimed, "How beautiful!" A little child observing the parade said, "He has got nothing on!"

The Princess and the Pea

A prince was looking for a real princess. It happened that during a heavy rainstorm a girl appeared at the town gate soaked with water. She said to the King who opened the gate that she was a real princess.

The Queen deciding to test the girl's statement took all the bedclothes off, laid a single pea on the bedstead then put 20 mattresses on top of it, and 20 feathers bedspreads on top of the mattresses.

The girl who claimed to be a princess said sleeping on top of the mattress was terrible.

"I seemed to be lying on something very hard!" she said.

Thus, the prince found his princess. The pea is now in a museum, if no one has stolen it.

Classical Literature

In the realm of classical literature, there is no greater fable than the one created by the Spanish author Miguel de Cervantes (1547 - 1616), who began writing the *Adventures of Don Quixote de la Mancha* while in jail.

It is the story of a man nearly fifty years old, bedecked with rusty armor and sword, and repaired helmet. He is astride his chosen horse, Rozimante, and loves a peasant girl nominated as "mistress of his heart" unbeknownst to her. He calls her Dulcinia.

Strengthened by a pretense ceremony conducted by a constable who gave him the title "knight errant," he is accompanied by his squire, a laborer neighbor and honest man, named Sancho Panza.

Don Quxiote was ready for the world of windmills and other marvelous beings.

Author Cervantes concluded his masterpiece with the words "the sold object of mine was to expose to the contempt they deserved the extravagant and silly tricks of Chivalry, which my true and generous Don Quixote has nearly accomplished. Their credit in the world being now actually tottering will doubtless sink altogether never to return again. Farewell."

The Great Fables of All Nations is an excellent presentation of fables selected by Manuel Komroff, including 345 of Aesop's best works, and introducing authors from France, Italy, Ireland, America, Germany, Spain and Russia whose works add a variety of perspective to the genre.

The three American authors included are Emerson (The Mountain and the Squirrel); Franklin (Apologue, The Ephemera; An Arabian Tale); and the Scottish-born transplant Robert Louis Stevenson (The Devil and the Innkeeper" The citizen and the Traveler; t The Penitent; The Side Man and the Fireman; The Reader; The Tadpole and the Frog; The Cart Horse and the Saddle Horse.)

James Thurber's *Fables for our Times* includes 28 fables such as "The Unicorn in the Garden." It is the exquisite story of a man who sees a White Unicorn with a golden horn in the middle of its forehead. The animal is cropping roses in the garden.

Excited by his discovery, the man rushes home and reports the wonderful event to his wife.

"You are a Booby," she says, and threatens to put him in the booby hatch.

After several such exchanges, the wife calls the police and a psychiatrist. They take her away, because the unicorn is a mythical beast. The man lived happily ever after.

Because this book is concerned about life on the Water Planet called Earth, it is fitting to conclude this chapter with an old fable, retold by Vivian French in the 1933 children's book, *Why the Sea is Salty*.

The author describes a magical churn which repays a little girl's generosity and the greedy actions of a covetous uncle. The churn produces whatever its owner wishes for, and the little girl receives it from a tiny, aged man who vanished in a puff of wind. A rich uncle snatches the churn away and flees to the sea, sailing away in his ship.

During his dinner, he commands the churn to provide him with salt to season his food, and realizes too late that he has no magic words to stop the churn. Salt pours out everywhere, eventually filling the ship, which sinks from the weight.

No one knows what happened to the uncle. The ship's crew rows to shore. The magic churn sinks to the bottom of the freshwater sea where it continues to produce a stream of salt. It is churning even today, and that is why the sea is salty.

Remember that 97.3% of earth's water is in the oceans. 2.1% is in ice caps and glaciers, and another 0.59% is in ground water.

Only .1% is found in rivers and lakes!

25

Shakespeare

All the world's a stage
And all the men and women merely players;
They have their exits and their entrances,
And one man in his time plays many parts...
  —Jacques: As You Like It *Act II, Scene VII*

There are two perspective which are especially helpful when viewing the literary treasure the English-speaking world has inherited from the Bard, William Shakespeare.

Perspective I: The plays, sonnets, poems and songs which have earned Shakespeare acclaim as the preeminent genius of English literature. It is genius not for an age, but for all time, the mirror in which we see our idealized selves.

Perspective II: The question pressed by many scholars is, who was William Shakespeare? Was the author Shakespeare, Shagspire, Shakspeare, Shaxpire – or none of the above? Was the genius who created the wondrous literature someone other than the man from Stratford-upon Avon? Was Shakespeare a protective, necessary pseudonym?

The writings of William Shakespeare are monumental; 37 plays, 154 sonnets, poems, and songs. When included in the

Globe Illustrated: Shakespeare the Complete Works Annotated they required 2,634 pages in 3 volumes with forward, preface, adjunctive, appendices, Shakespeare's will, account of his life, commendatory verses. The *Globe* is a book 4 inches thick, 8.5 by 11 inches, weighing 8 pounds. It is visually intimidating, despite a beautiful presentation, and is edited by Howard Stanton with commentaries by Samuel Coleridge and Samuel Johnson. Illustrations are by Sir Gilbert and Ray Ebel. Engravings are by the brothers Dalgiel.

My copy of *The Globe* is shelved in the center of my small library. In size it dominates other volumes just as the plays, sonnets, poems and songs dominate English literature. I can not help but compare it with the "magical box" of Pandora, and recall that Hope was the one element that did not escape when she opened her god-given dowry treasure. For me, when I open *The Globe*, there is hope the world can discuss, appreciate and embrace the cultural icon that is inherent in Shakespeare's writings.

It isn't surprising that many researchers dispute the claim that William Shakespeare of Stratford-on-Avon was the same genius who authored the masterful plays, sonnets, poems, and songs. It is not these materials that are challenged, it is the authorship which is challenged, questioned, and debated.

The disputation has a curious parallel: the DWEM's (Dead, White European Males) domination in world affairs. Consider the parallel of Shakespeare, cultural icon of English literature and the jewel of Spanish Literature, Miguel de Cervantes.

Stratford-on-Avon, Shakespeare's birthplace (1564) has been described as a squalid, bookless neighborhood of some 1,500 persons. John Shakespeare, William's father, was active in grain and malt businesses, and was described in the Bailiff's Register as a glover (one who makes gloves) engaged in agricultural pursuits. He is also described as a butcher and a dealer in wool. Records also disclose he served as constable, chamberlain, bailiff, and alderman.

In contrast, little is known of John Shakespeare's son William. He may have attended a free school in Stratford (there are no records, however). In 1582, William Shakespeare, age eighteen, married Anne Hathaway, (eight years his senior). They had three children. Tradition has it that William quit his home and family because of an incident in which he and other youths were caught poaching deer from the park of Sir Thomas Lucy. Young Shakespeare may have composed a harsh lampoon in retribution for his punishment that brought further persecution from Sir Lucy.

It is reported this drove Shakespeare to leave his family about 1586. He went to London, arriving without money or friends. It is surmised Shakespeare initially found work at some theater in London, possibly in a mean task such as caring for the gentleman's horses while they attended the play.

Perhaps young Shakespeare first joined the group playing at Blackfriar's Theatre. Later, perhaps in 1594, he is thought to have played in the Globe, located on the South bank of the Thames.

In Howard Stanton's preface to *The Globe*, he notes that the personal history of Shakespeare is so little known "that it is impossible to say who made provision for the publication of this transcendent work." Later, Stanton points out that of all the poems and plays – or fragments of either – with the exception of five or six cases "not a word in his handwriting is known to exist."

Any serious consideration of the question "Who was Shakespeare?" must be based upon the times and the social, political, and religious environment of 16th century England. It was a time dominated by the tempestuous reign of Queen Elizabeth (1558-1603).

In the first year of Queen Elizabeth's rule, the Invincible Armada of Spain's King Phillip II sailed against England with 130 ships and 30,000 men. Queen Elizabeth donned armor and pronounced herself to be "a weak and feeble woman, but with the heart and stomach of a King."

With her small navy and the assistance of adventurer Sir Francis Drake, the Spanish Armada was crushed (a violent storm also aided the English seamen).

England's fortunes rose. Renaissance fever raised cultural and commercial levels; brilliant authors, painters, and craftsmen flourished. Commerce and industry strengthened the world of arts, and the theater – especially in London – flourished.

For years, actors had played their roles in public places wherever space permitted and a crowd could be attracted. Private performances (free of common folk) were welcomed in palaces and in the halls of nobility. Scenery, props, and dressing rooms were scant. A theater was virtually unknown until about 1576, when a carpenter named James Burbage built London's first.

Too, the world was rough for the actors. Titled nobles and well-to-do persons looked down upon actors as an irresponsible, scoundrel-like lot. Puritan clergy denounced the plays as sinful events that turned righteous people away from their prayers.

Fortunately, such was not the judgment of the common people, who crowded the new theater and vocally applauded and harassed the players. The actors joined groups that flourished under the sponsorship of patrons and took the stage with sponsor names such as the "King's Men" and "Lord Chamberlain's Men."

There is little information about Burbage's first theater building or about other early theater. The best data have been supplied by a Dutchman, Johannes de Witt, who in 1596 visited the great Swan Theatre, built to accommodate some 3,000 theatre-goers. It was de Witt who made interior and exterior sketches of the Swan.

In 1613, The Globe burned to the ground. A cannon was fired and the roof caught fire, bringing down the house. After a quick rebuild, the Globe continued performances until 1642, when it was demolished.

A brewery occupied the spot until 1894, when the land was used as a parking lot. Some 400 years later, the Globe was rebuilt, opening for performances on June 12, 1987.

It is interesting to note that theater, actors, playwrights, and theatre-goers have had strongly convoluted relationships with the government.

1594 saw London's aldermen barring playhouses in the city. In 1642, Puritan leadership shut down the theater for a period of twenty years.

The entire world of theater of the 1500s and 1600s presented major differences from our present day concepts. Women were not to act in public; their roles were played by boys. Performances were held every day except Sunday, and shows were offered in the afternoons from 2 to 5 pm. There were no evening performances (no electricity), and there were no intermissions. Advertising of theatrical performance was not permitted, resulting in the flying of flags that announced stage content by color. A white flag signaled comedy, red was raised for history, and black for tragedy. Trumpets sounded for the events each afternoon. Sometimes fear of an impending plague would close the theater.

How different it is today. Theaters are luxurious symbols of cultural wealth. Actors are honored iconic figures. Stratford-on-Avon is a target for tourist and theater-goers (three Shakespearean playhouses). The Royal Shakespeare Company represents the world's leading repertory system.

In the February 1959 issue of the *American Bar Association Journal*, an article entitled "Elizabethan Whodunit: Who was William Shakespeare?" encouraged the *Journal*'s readers to respond with pro and con letters about the authorship of the plays, sonnets, and poems attributed to William Shakespeare of Stratford-on-Avon.

Richard Bentley, author of the article, died in 1970. He and former editor-in-chief Tappan Gregory had joined to produce the first printing of the trade magazine and are remembered for their decision to initiate such a seminal discussion for lawyers.

Gregory defended the article's inclusion as "one of evidence, and therefore within the providence of lawyers."

The small book *Shakespeare Cross Examination* was the result of the letters generated by the magazine article and was published by the *American Bar Association Journal*.

Nine original articles and 32 excerpts from letters are included in the slim book, lightweight at 10 ounces compared to the monster *The Globe*. (Side by side on my book shelf, these two books seem to be symbols of David and Goliath.)

Bentley's question about the identity of the Bard brought out some facts from readers.

- known facts about Shakespeare are few;
- first real biography published 93 years after Shakespeare's death;
- no direct proof of authorship of plays, sonnets;
- Shakespeare's will, no mention of theater, writings;
- three will signatures, none spelled Shakespeare;
- left wife (in will) with second best bed with furniture;
- no manuscript extant proved to be Shakespeare;
- none of Shakespeare's contemporaries refer to him as writer;
- no record of Shakespeare's schooling;
- no evidence of travel abroad nor familiarity with Greek, Latin or current foreign languages; no evidence of Court or Socials circles.

Author Bentley raises the question, in light of foregoing factors: How could such a person have a 15,000 word vocabulary and knowledge of Greek, Latin and legal proceedings? Bentley suggests that Shakespeare was a genius.

Charles Dickens was quoted as pointing out that "the life of William Shakespeare is a great mystery."

Three candidates proposed by Bentley as worthy of consideration as the "real" Shakespeare include Francis Bacon, Christopher Marlowe, and Edward de Vere.

Francis Bacon (1561-1626) was a Cambridge scholar who was admitted to the Bar at age 21, later knighted and served as solicitor general and attorney general.

Christopher Marlowe (1564-1593) was also a graduate of Cambridge University, considered by some as the greatest discoverer, and the most daring and inspired pioneer in all poetic literature. His reported murder on May 30, 1593, has been conjectured as a ruse to permit Marlowe to escape and hide abroad.

Edward de Vere (1550-1604) was 17th Earl of Oxford, a Cambridge and Oxford graduate, and the producer of poetry and plays. He founded the actor's troupe called Oxford's Boys.

Why the anonymity? One possible answer could be in the unwritten code which forbade publication of poetry produced by nobility during their lives.

Author Bentley quoted Sigmund Freud's belief that the works attributed to Shakespeare were likely written by another with Shakespeare as a penname.

"I am almost convinced," wrote Freud, "that the assumed name concealed the personality of Edward de Vere, Earl of Oxford."

Eight responses follow Bentley's presentation in the book.

1. "A Mystery Solved: The True Identity of Shakespeare" by Charlton Ogburn, who concludes "there is no record of [Shakespeare's] having attended school. There is not a scintilla of evidence that he was ever identified by anyone as William Shakespeare, the poet and dramatist."

2. "The Case for the Defense: Deere et al vs. Shakespeare" by William W. Clary, who proposed there are "good reasons why a lawyer may rest in the belief that the much maligned man of Stratford, not withstanding his lawsuits and his dealing in malt, was the man whodunit." The three other men are shown to have been members of a company of players, Clary concludes, and "official records show that a man named Will Shakespeare was a member of their company."

3. "The Shakespeare Controversy: A Stratfordian Rejoinder" by John N. Hauser, who wrote that "the anti-Stratfordian case rests on a series of premises that Shakespeare of Stratford came from a background of illiteracy, was himself illiterate and unschooled and went unnoticed as a writer. These premises can not be sustained. They are contrary to fact or at best unsupported by the evidence. There were many contemporary references to Shakespeare."

4. "The True Shakespeare: England's Great and Complete Man" by Dorothy and Charlton Ogburn (authors of *The Renaissance Man of England* and *This Star of England*) who wrote that "ten facts [exist] fundamental to recognition of the identity of Shakespeare as Edward de Vere, 17th Earl of Oxford." The leading fact, they claim, is that the poet dramatist was forced to be anonymous and that is the heart of his mystery, that "his name was concealed" and buried.

5. "Francis Bacon and the Knights of the Helmet," by Commander Martin Pares, R.N., who pointed out that "at Gray's Inn, Bacon was a member of the Order of the Helmet, symbolizing invisibility and dedicated to Pallas Athene, the Shaker of the Spear." Pares emphasized that "Bacon was the moving spirit in promoting the Act of Union between England and Scotland, and he was on the council of the first Virginia Company."

6. "Did Shaxper Write Shakespeare?" by Arthur E. Briggs, who analyzes the "dropout print" of Shakespeare's first folio, a print commonly purposed to be a likeness of Shakespeare. Briggs observed that the clothing in the image is such that "no tailor would have designed and no one but a clown would have worn. The two sides do not match." In describing biographical data concerning William Shaxper, author Briggs notes data abound, but relying on "such expressions as "if so," "possibly," "it seems," "may have," "must have," and "probably."

7. "Marlowe's Might Line: Was Marlowe Murdered at Twenty Nine?" by Benjamin Wham, who questioned the

story of Marlowe's murder at age 29. Wham notes that Marlowe was charged with atheism and his former room mate, Kyd, had been tortured on the rack. His friend, Francis Kett, had been burned at the stake "for no greater charges. Marlowe's position was desperate." Wham contends that Marlowe escaped to the Continent, spent time in hiding, and returned to an anonymous existence.

8. "A Hoax Three Centuries Old," by Louis P. Benezer, who says Edward de Vere was admitted to Cambridge University "when he was 9 years old, had an A.B. before he was fourteen, and M.A. at 16, and L.L.B before he was 19." During these years, Oxford leased the Blackfriar's Theatre.

The treasure-trove we call the plays, sonnets, songs, and poems of Shakespeare are our literary heritage. Whether created by William Shakespeare, Francis Bacon, Christopher Marlowe, Edward de Vere, or some other genius, we can rejoice in our heritage.

And what did that genius say of his homeland?

This royal throne of kings, this sceptered isle,
This earth of majesty, this seat of mars,
This other Eden, demi-paradise...
This happy breed of men, this little world,
This precious Stone, set in the silver sea...
This blessed plot, this earth, this realm,
This England..."
    —Richard II; John of Gaunt, Act II, Scene I.

And Shakespeare's words for all persons?

This above all: to thine own self be true,
And it must follow, as the night the day,
Thou canst not be false to any man.
    —Hamlet: Act I Scene III, Polonius Advice to Laertes.

26

Vaudeville

With the fearful strain that is on me night and day, if I did not laugh, I should die.
   —Abraham Lincoln (1809 - 1865)

Given the uncertainties and burdens introduced to all Americans September 11th, actions tragically repetitive of the preemptive strike at Pearl Harbor, Lincoln's admission that laughter is life-saving serves as a direct personal prescription for survival. Seeking laughter for personal relief, and for survival, has been significant — again and again — in cultural renewal and strength.

Normandy, France, introduced Europe to the *Chansons du Vau de Vire,* or Songs of the Valley of Vire, from which we have inherited the word Vaudeville. Satirical couplets on political topics emerged in the 1400s. It is thought that French poet Olivie Basselin authored some of the songs most favored by the village people.

In England, in the 1500s through the 1800s, actors practiced their art wherever a public place gave them a stage to offer their dramas, poems, and songs.

In the new world of America, from perhaps 1875 to 1925, vaudeville held full sway and popularity. In an outstanding work by Charles and Louise Samuels, *The Merry World of Vaudeville* it is noted there were 25,000 artists working part or full time. These artists roamed the country presenting their skills in astonishing variety whenever an audience could be gathered. There were perhaps 4,000 stages in venues that ranged from barns and makeshift outdoor stages to lodge halls and ultimately, palatial buildings.

These popular entertainment movements, from the 1400s to the 1900s, provided waves of cultural relief from tension and created avenues for strengthened community inter-relationships. The wave from Normandy is a similar wave of theater from England, and our own American wave in the rough jokes and patter. Minstrel shows and vaudeville, the songs, dances, acts, and acrobatic antics, all were evidence of the healing power of the "people's art."

Despite the people's joy, the life of actors, troubadours, and minstrels, was initially difficult. For example, London's theater life was the west bank of the Thames, condemned constantly by government fiat. Religious groups considered the theater and its actors as sinners, undesirables, riffraff or worse.

In America, early vaudeville actors were similarly regarded as a scruffy crew, but the need to release from society's stressful existence and the need for laughter's comfort, gave life to the world of vaudeville. An early feature was the minstrel show, generally a troupe of white comedians in blackface presenting songs, jokes, and short skits. The name minstrel is derived from an old French term that originally meant servant. America's early vaudeville actors were seldom held in high esteem.

It is significant that one of the outstanding characteristics of these early traveling artists was their individuality. It was their act, their singular performance, their words, and their original concepts, presented on their own, singing with or without a partner. Every performance was without outside direction or prompting. There were a few retakes and whatever it took, they did it themselves.

Additionally it was a world in which most had more than one histrionic skill; singing, dancing, reciting, and performing were all parts of the total package presented by vaudevillians.

Accomplished self-taught individuals were sustained by artistic instinct: double in brass, VTR (Vamp Til Ready), and always leave 'em laughing.

The life of Vaudeville in America spanned some sixty years. During that time span, many of the country's most skillful and gifted performers participated, honing their talents through the rigorous circuits of vaudeville. The names bring back many memories: Ed Wynn, Buster Keaton, Al Jolson, Harry Lauder, Oscar Levant, Ray Bolger, Lillian Russell. Many will remember Sophie Tucker (*Some of These Days*) Louise Dresser (*My Gal Sal*), The Dolly Sisters, Nora Bayes, Mae West, and Hildegarde.

The list is as long as your memories: Bert Williams, Oscar Hammerstein, Will Rogers, Jack Benny, Eddie Foy, Eddie Cantor, the Marx Brothers, George Jessel, George M. Cohan, Milton Berle, Bob Hope, and Bing Crosby.

Vaudeville slowly relinquished the responsibility of offering laughter and song and dance to palatial theater, radio, and movies. It was a gradual diminution of America's original live theater.

Today as re-runs of the best TV stations offer stand-up performers in *I Love Lucy*, and the *Lawrence Welk Show*, both classic reminders of acts and songs of yesteryear and the music, dances, and skits of vaudeville inheritance.

If you are old enough to occasionally wish for the good old days, or intellectually emotionally aware and stimulated by yesteryear's theatric treasures, the recipe for laughter still exists. A special example is the Plaza Theatre in the heart of downtown Palm Springs, California.

My wife and I attended the tenth anniversary of the *Palm Springs Follies* held at the Plaza. What a deluge of irresistible songs! "There's no business like Show Business," "Sunny side of the Street," "Hello, Dolly!" "Mary is a Grand Old Name," "Let me call you Sweetheart," "You, You Beautiful Doll,"

"Ain't We Got Fun?" "My Baby Just Cares for Me," "I've got the World on a String." The guest star feature was the much anticipated return engagement of Anne Maria Albergetti.

Creators of the *Palm Springs Follies*, theatrical professional Riff Markowitz and Mary Jardin, visualized their *Follies* as "one of the best of the best." The cast consisted of professional, first-rate performers, who just happen to be old. The *Palm Springs Follies* are "about second chances and the miracle of these people having fond theirs," said the producers. "We're in the business of giving hope."

These concepts become meaningful when you learn the eleven famous long-legged lovelies ranged in age from 57 to 83. Jill Gordon believes "age is a great opportunity for growth!" Beverly Allen adds: "Keep moving, keep learning, keep smiling!"

The six-man Dashing Dandies ranged in age from 56 to 73 in the anniversary performance. 73-year-old Jerry Antes claims, "The older you get the better it was!"

The 2005 vaudeville and burlesque style *Follies*, held in the historic Plaza Theatre (a theatre which has presented such performers as Frank Sinatra, Bing Crosby, Pearl Bailey, Jack Benny, Don Ameche, Donald O'Connor, Kay Starr, the Mills Brothers, Gloria de Haven, and Jo Ann Castel) spotlighted The Four Aces, Fred Diodati (age 74), Joe Giglio (age 64), Joe Amato (age 59), and Harry Heisler (age 59).

Sharing the spotlight were plate-spinner Leonardo Menna (age 75), and King of the Ventriloquists Sammy Kieg (age 64), with Francisco, a huge, witty, wise-cracking parrot of undetermined age.

The stage and the desire to perform remain. It is not curtain and exeunt. Tomorrow's world of theater and laughter, the universe of song and dance and patter, continues inexpressibly.

All over the U.S. the love for theater, for live performance, and for the action of expression is evident. Theatrical energies are everywhere in our schools. As Edward Bulwer observed: "There is that in theatrical representation which awakens whatever romance belongs to our character the magic lights; the pomp of scene, the fair, false, exciting life that is detailed before us."

In 2005, in a crowded public school auditorium, several hundred parents, students, teachers, and administrators all enthusiastically focused their attention on the thespians, musicians, dancers, artists, and vocalists about to present their version of Rogers and Hammerstein's acclaimed "Cinderella."

This particular theatrical event, a happy musical adventure set in a wonderland of myth, was held in Southern California under the auspices of a network of supportive organizations. Included were the high school, the unified school district, the associated student body, the drama club, the performing arts department, and the Interact Club.

A cast of 11 character actors, 25 chorus members, and 32 special performers enacted in such roles as horses, mice, fairies, floral designs, cooks, dessert servers, and tapestry sellers. All of these, including the members of the orchestra, were central contributors to the total performance.

Additionally many individuals served in less-recognized but very necessary supportive activities. 20 aided with arrangements and logistics, transportation, and prop building (including the design and construction of the elaborate pumpkin carriage), backstage assistants, make-up, hair and costuming, ticket assistance, ushering, and printing. 17 additional assistants worked at set and backdrop construction.

All of these participants contributed, assisted in presenting the conjunctive total of their expertise via the age-old medium of theater: music, song, dance, skits, and acting. It was a wondrous adventure into another world of storied myth, yesteryear and tomorrow-land, preserving and presaging laughter and hope for society.

27

Poetry

*Monsieur Jordan was delighted to learn that he had been
speaking prose all his life.*
—Jean-Baptiste Poquelin, his stage name, Molière*

Molière is the *nom de plume* of Jean Baptiste Poquelin. Like his contemporary William Shakespeare, many of his theatre writings were recognized as masterpieces of poetic literature. Similarly, Shakespeare employed metrical forms and rhythmic patterns which generally distinguish poetry from prose.

It is interesting to reflect upon the reception of Shakespeare's "Venus and Adonis," a poem that quickly became the most popular in England and remained so for years. 15 printings were completed between 1593 and 1636, representing more attention than his plays received in that period.

"Venus and Adonis" was Shakespeare's first published poem and was introduced in the first six verses with the following lines:

*She red and hot as coals of glowing fire,
He red for shame, but frosty in desire.*

About three centuries before the publication of "Venus and Adonis," the Persian astronomer and poet Omar Khayyam (Khayyam signifies tent maker; a trade in which it is reported he worked in his early years) produced a series of some 200 quatrains which drew acclaim throughout the world. The simplicity of the quatrain structure, usually four lines with alternate rhyme, is evidenced in his justification of pantheism:

> *If I myself a lesser creed*
> *Have loosely strung the Jewel of Good deed,*
> *Let this one thing for my atonement plead*
> *That one for two I never did mis-read*

As a scientist, Khayyam assisted the Sultanate in reforming his country's calendar. In his search for meaning in the drama of the universe, he described the pleasures of the senses as the nexus for a serious pursuit of the meaning of life. He put forth such a pursuit in his *Rubiyat of Omar Khayyam.*

> *A book of verses underneath the bough,*
> *A jug of wine, a loaf of bread and Thou*
> *Beside me singing in the wilderness...*
> *Oh wilderness were paradise now!*

Perhaps Omar Khayyam's most famous contribution to philosophic poetry is:

> *The moving finger writes: and having write,*
> *Moves on; nor all your piety and wit*
> *Shall lure it back to cancel half a line,*
> *Nor all your tears wash out a word of it.*

Slightly more contemporary is "The Daffodils" by William Wordsworth:

> *I wandered lonely as a cloud*
> *That floats on high o'er vales and hills,*
> *When all at once I saw a crowd,*
> *A host of golden daffodils,*
> *Beside the lake, beneath the trees,*
> *Fluttering and dancing in the breeze.*

Wordsworth approached pragmatic (generally peace-dominated) subjects with equal poetic softness: "Sonnet" is introduced with two philosophic lines:

> *The world is too much with us; late and soon,*
> *Getting and spending, we lay waste our powers:*

In a somewhat similar pensive philosophic mood, John Milton described his heavy personal burden in "Sonnet on His Blindness:"

> *When I consider how my light is spent*
> *Ere half my days, in this dark world and wide,*
> *And that one talent, which is death to hide,*
> *Lodged with me useless..."*

Not all poetic writings were confined to such serious philosophic issues; humor and excitement are prime subjects. Oliver Wendell Holmes' "The Deacon's Masterpiece" is a rollicking story about a carriage that captures the tone and laughs about a world before automobiles:

> *Have you hear of the wonderful one-horse shay*
> *That was built in such a logical way*
> *It ran a hundred years to a day,*

Can there be a more exciting introduction to the world of the holiday season than "The Night Before Christmas," by Clement Clarke Moore?

> *'Twas the night before Christmas,*
> *When all through the house,*
> *Not a creature was stirring.*
> *Not even a mouse.*

Poet Eugene Field also brought humor and excitement together in his Christmas story:

> *Most all the time, the whole year round,*
> *There ain't no flies on me,*
> *But jest 'fore Christmas, I'm as good as I can be!*

The wonderful excitement of traveling to visit a cherished relative is captured in an exquisite poem, "Out to Old Aunt Mary's," by James Whitcomb Riley. These lines are poetic jewels:

> *And the long highway, with sunshine spread*
> *As thick as butter on country bread.*
> *Our cares behind, and our hearts ahead.*

The theme of highways is employed by Sam Walter Foss in his "The House by the Side of the Road," based on the poetic insight of the Greek epic poet Homer's lines: *He was a friend to man, and he lived in a house by the side of the road.* Foss exclaims: *Let me live in a house by the side of the road and be a friend to man.*

Perhaps a relevant conclusion to this section may be found in the poem "Soliture" by Ella Wheeler Wilcox:

> *Laugh and the world laughs with you:*
> *Weep, and you weep alone.*

There is no better way to understand the significant difference between prose and poetry than to reflect upon the subject of trees. In "dictionary prose," tree may be described as a perennial plant having a permanent woody self-supporting main stem or trunk, ordinarily growing to considerable height. The tree family produces the tallest living objects on our planet.

To a scientist documenting genetic engineering in plants and absorbed with research on the ability of trees to absorb and neutralize ground based contaminants, trees are a basis for a new agricultural revolution, a partial answer to world hunger.

The pioneer in this field, Milton P. Gordon, was a professor at the University of Washington and associate editor of *Biochemistry Journal*. He died in 2005.

Now listen to the poet's description of trees. Joyce Kilmer observed:

> *I think that I shall never see*
> *A poem lovely as a tree.*

Henry C. Bunner asks in "The Heart of the Tree"

> *What does he plant who plants a tree?*
> *He plants a friend of sun and sky;*
> *He plants the flag of breezes free;*
> *The shaft of beauty, towering high.*

Edna St. Vincent Millay voices a glorious question in 'The Leaf and the Tree:"

> *When will you learn myself to be*
> *a dying leaf on a living tree?*
> *Shall not these branches in the end*
> *To wisdom and the truth ascend?*

On a formal note, Edwin Markham paid homage to

Lincoln, the man of the people:

His words were oaks in acorns and his thoughts were roots that firmly gripped the granite truth.

Among poetic exclamations of philosophic import, several are illustrative. In "Each and All", Ralph Waldo Emerson declares:

All are needed by each one
Nothing is fair or good alone.

Again, on being asked "whence is the flower," Emerson writes in "The Rhodora:"

Tell them dear, that if eyes were made for seeing,
then beauty is its own excuse for being.

In "The Builders," Longfellow describes our fate:

All are architects of Fate
Working in these walls of time
some with massive deeds and great,
Some with ornament of rhyme.

William Henley asserts in "Invictus:"

Out of the night that covers me
I think whatever gods may be
for my unconquerable soul.

Our lives are described by James Russell Lowell in "June" (the vision of Sir Launfal) in this fashion:

Daily with souls that cringe and plot,
We Sinais climb and know it not.

Almost as if in anticipatory response to Mohandas Ghandi's observation "An eye for an eye, and we all go blind," and as if in need to understand the strange biblical silence following the passage "Pilate saith unto him, 'What is truth?'" Poet John Keats penned these words for the closing lines of "Ode on a Grecian Urn:"

> "Beauty is truth, truth beauty" — that is all
> Ye know on earth, and all ye need to know.

In addition to Keats and Ghandi, poet Emily Dickinson envisions a comprehensive response to eye-for-eye blindness and biblical silence to "What is Truth?" Her vision is offered with her poem "1129" in the concluding lines:

> The truth must dazzle gradually
> or every man be blind.

I know of no more perceptive insight into natural human perversity then Robert Frost's "Mending Wall:"

> Something there is that doesn't love wall,
> that wants it down. I could say Elves to him,
> But it's not elves exactly, and I'd rather
> he said it for himself.

Nature's reality and beauty encouraged Edna St. Vincent Millay to write, in "Renascence:"

> All I could see from where I stood
> was three long mountains and a wood
> and further:
> The world stands our on either side
> No wider than the heart is wide.

There are poetic images in poetry to accommodate almost every mood. Here are thoughtful lines from a masterful poet:

For all sad words of tongue or pen
the saddest are these: it might have been.
    —John Greenlieaf Whittier: "Maud Muller."

For a change of perspective and concept, consider several poems about patriotism and war. In "America For Me," Henry Van Dyke proudly describes:

In the land of youth and freedom
beyond the oceans bars,
Where the air is full of sunlight
and the flag is full of stars

Lieutenant Colonel John McCrae wrote "In Flanders Fields:"

In Flanders Fields the poppies blow
Between the crosses, row on row.

And later:

We are the dead. Short days ago
We lived, felt dawns saw sunset glow.

Lastly:

Take up our quarrel with the foe.

In his poem, "Grass," Carl Sandburg pleads:

Pick up the bodies high
at Austerlitz and Waterloo
Shove them under and let me work.

It would not be thoughtful, it would not be appreciated, if brief note of the poetic power, cadence, rhythmic beat and flow of the text in the authorized King James version of the Bible was not include in this brief commentary.

> *And the earth was without form and void:*
> *and darkness was upon the face of the deep*
> —Genesis 1.2

> *So God created man in his own image,*
> *in the image of God created he him;*
> *male and female created he them.*
> —Genesis; 1 - 27

> *but where shall wisdom be found?*
> *And where is the place of understanding:*
> —Job 28-12

> *Ask, and it shall be given you;*
> *seek, and ye shall find;*
> *Knock and it shall be opened unto you*
> —Matthew: 7-7

This entire book is dedicated by virtue of its title to an appreciation for the waters of this planet. Poets have paid homage to rivers, lakes, seas, oceans. Here are a few of their acknowledgments:

John Masefield: "Sea Fever"

> *I must go down to the seas again,*
> *to the lovely sea and the sky.*

William Cullen Bryant: "Thanatopsis:

> *In majesty and the complaining brooks,*
> *that make the meadows green; and poured round*
> *Old ocean's gray and melancholy waste.*

Alfred Tennyson: "Crossing the Bar:"

> *Sunset and evening star,*
> *and one clear call for me*
> *And may there be moaning of the bar*
> *When I put out to sea.*

"Childe Harold's Pilgrimage," by George Gordon, Lord Byron:

> *Roll on thou deep and dark blue ocean, roll!*
> *Then thousand fleets sweep over there in vain.*

Henry Wadsworth Longfellow: "Hiawatha's Childhood

> *Bright before it beat the water*
> *Beat the clear and sunny water,*
> *Beat the shining big-sea water.*

Cincinnatus Miller (Joaquin Miller): "Columbus":

> *Behind him lay the gray Azores,*
> *Behind the Gates of Hercules;*
> *Before him not the ghost of shores*
> *before him only shoreless seas.*

Sidney Lanier: Song of the Chattahoochee;"

> *Out of the hills of Habersham*
> *Down the valleys of Hall,*
> *I hurry amain to reach the plain,*
> *Run the rapid and leap the fall.*

It would be well to turn our attention to poetry's joy in humor such as that found in Holmes' "The Deacon's Masterpiece," Eugene Field's "Jest 'fore Christmas. Several other examples of outstanding treatment include Lewis

Carroll's "You are Old, Father William." It is considered a masterpiece of nonsense verse, based on an earlier poem by Robert Southey. An example of this adaptation by Carroll:

> *In my youth, said the father,*
> *I took to the law,*
> *And argued each case with my wife:*
> *and the muscular strength.*
> *Which it gave to my jaw,*
> *Has lasted the rest of my life.*

On of the most famous poems in Carroll's *Through the Looking Glass,* "Jabberwocky:"

> *Twas brillig, and the slithy toves*
> *Did gyre and gimble in the wabe:*
> *All mimsey were the borogoves,*
> *and the mome raths outgrabe.*

Whatever you may think, it rhymes and is world famous.
Another of Carroll's poetic no-nonsense masterpieces, "The Walrus and the Carpenter," contains these lines:

> *The time has come, the Walrus said*
> *To talk of many thing:*
> *Of shoes and ships and sealing wax*
> *of cabbages and kings.*

"Lewis Carroll" is the pen name of Rev. Charles Lutwidge Dodgson. His fame rests upon "Alice's Adventures in Wonderland" and "Through the Looking Glass." His terminal poem in the second volume contains an exquisite three lines:

> *Ever drifting down the stream*
> *Lingering in the golden Gleam*
> *Life, what is it but a dream?*

A unique source of poetic whimsy appeared in a newspaper column "The Sun Dial," which ran for years in the *New York Sun*. The major characters were Archy (a cockroach), who had been a free verse bard in a former life, and Mehitabel (a cat whose former life experience, she claimed, had been that of Cleopatra). Fascinated readers of the column followed the adventures of Archy and Mehitabel avidly.

How did Archy, the poet, produce his stories? By climbing at night on a reporter's typewriter, jumping head-first on key after key. It was slow, but he was obdurate and hardheaded. There could be no capital letters; line shifting was also not possible. His readers understood. Early on, he typed this explanation:

> *expression is the need of my soul*
> *I was once a vers libre bard*
> *but I died and my soul went into*
> *the body of a cockroach*
> *it has given me a new outlook on life*

Mehitalel the cat often sang these lines, according to archy:

> *there is a dance in the old dame yet*
> *toujours gai archy toujours gai*

A special character in Archy's stories had to do with Warty Bliggins, a philosophic toad. Archy described Warty's position:

> *do not tell me*
> *said warty bliggins*
> *that there is not a purose*
> *in the universe*
> *the thought is blasphemy*

Let's look briefly at two major poems of nationalism. Australia's national anthem contains these poetic lines:

> *For those who come across the seas*
> *We've boundless plains to share*
> *With courage let us all embrace*
> *To advance Australia's Fair."*

American's Statue of Liberty bears the poem "The New Colossus," written by Emma Lazarus. The statue is the centerpiece of Liberty Island, (formerly Bedloe's Island). The American Museum of Immigration was opened in 1972 at the base of the statue. The 14-line poem by Emma Lazarus concludes with these words:

> *Give me your tired, your poor,*
> *Your huddled masses yearning to be free,*
> *The wretched refuse of your teeming shore.*
> *Send these, the homeless tempest tossed to me,*
> *I lift my lamp beside the golden door.*

National poetry can be inspiring. Too, by selective silence, it can be the symbol of tragedy. Neither Australia's poetic national anthem, nor America's poetry enhanced Colossus of Liberty are concerned with the indigenous peoples whose lands are appropriated, who right to participate in government were extirpated and whose populations were savagely decimated with "genocidic" fervor. Poetry can house the same dangers; can avoid responsibility for brotherhood, with all the efficiency of prose.

There are poems which seem to embrace all life with warm assurance of hope for all mankind, gentle, compassionate expression that all is well.

Robert Browning's Pippa Passes:

The year's at the spring..
And day's at the morn.
Morning's at seven
The hillside dew pearled;

The Lark's on the wing
The Snail on the thorn;
God's in his Heaven...
All's right with the world.

It is the intuitive genius of poets such as Browning that touches our need for encouragement, for assurance. Indeed, why not draw sustenance, from warm, welcome words,

With the previous inclusion of poems concerned with patriotism and war, together with the discussion about distinguishing prose and poetry, I feel compelled to present a poem which was instrumental in securing "First Prize" at the Southern Intercollegiate Oratorical Championships in 1938.

Entitled "Brass Checks," the 18 quatrains were wrapped with 13 prose paragraphs. Together, poetry and prose advocated "No more War." Conductively, they proved to be a highly successful communicative device. (I cannot resist describing the problem "Brass Checks" presented the contest judges due to the use of an unattributed poem was used. When the orator replied, "That poem was written by me!" the judges expressed great surprise and apologized, and announced Dexter MacBride was the first prize winner.)

Herewith, are several quatrains from "Brass Checks."

They all wear these brass checks,
Thousands upon thousands of boys
many have volunteered service
And other the country employs.

There are million there like him
on one side or another,
And by a little brass check
He's another man's brother.

Millions of brass checks
Lying in ruts;
Bayoneted brass checks
Ripping out guts.

We won't come home on stretchers
As half-mangled half-human wrecks
All they'll do in the next war
Is send home our little brass checks.

In the decades that have passed since I created and presented "Brass Checks," vast changes have pounded perception and perspectives. The major emphasis of my poem – Death – now reveals I failed to understand the horror of casualties. True, acknowledged are "half-mangled half-human wrecks," but the enormous hurt, sorrow, and needs of wounded survivors was beyond my experience or comprehension. They are beyond the knowledge, experience, and comprehension of many Americans today.

Consider that returning veterans face many long-lasting and painful experiences related to employment and housing. The director of the U.S. Veterans Homeless Program, Peter Dougherty, was quoted in 2004 as saying "traditionally, what happens to you after you leave has not been of concern to the service."

The Veterans Administration faces a staggering task and struggles to keep up with five million veterans enrolled. Since the Afghanistan and Iraq wars an ever-increasing number of troops have been wounded in action. Undersecretary for Health Dr. J.J. Kussman says that times have changed since the Vietnam War, and the agency has spent $3.3 billion per year on mental health, adding $300 million for soldiers returning from Iraq and Afghanistan.

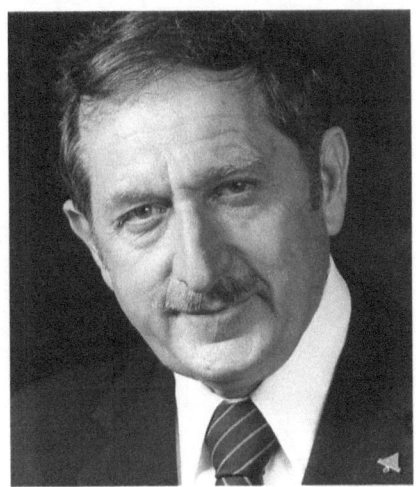

Dexter MacBride

The Army's Disabled Soldier support system is reported to be run by fewer than 10 people on a budget of $1 million in 2004. A spokesperson for paralyzed veterans believes the strain upon a system under extreme pressure doesn't end with veterans going to Walter Reed Army Medical Center in Washington, and then being treated. This is a life-long situation for them for the next 60 or so years.

So is the system going to be ready to serve them for all these years? That is the question.

In a discussion regarding homeless veterans, California U.S. Congressman Gary C. Miller shared with me his concern that "about one third of the adult homeless population has served [their country]. Veterans are living on the streets or in shelters."

According to government figures, veterans constitute 9% of the U.S. population, but 23% of the homeless populations.

Neither prose nor poetry can anesthetize the pain of war.

The Golden Arches

A strong presence in societal fabric.

Fabric is any material consisting of a string of connected parts; structure. A structure consists of relations between ideas, expressions, emotions, or the like. Societal fabrics at local, national, and global levels contain major interwoven threads of custom and precedent. Layer upon layer, society creates its interwoven threads extending the avenues and realms of human activity.

This layered world of human cognition is evident everywhere. Consider several principal threads.

Religion: massive, major yarns, interlaced upon devotional looms.

Law: whether interwoven with formal religious or emanating from civil government bodies, the thrust of the law is interwoven with every thread of societal fabrics.

Economics: despite the early concept of economics, today's world is dominated by the pragmatic approach that includes production, distribution, consumption of goods and services, and the material welfare of mankind.

Militarism: another massive, major thread in societal fabrics evaluated as imperative in national independence and survival. World War I caused an estimated 10 million combat deaths.

Health: because of global concern, health and survival is emerging as a significant thread in the fabric of society. The WWI years saw the pandemic of Spanish Flu and a reported 40 million deaths.

Transportation: mobility, accelerated by the automobile, produced vast, intricate threads of roadways, and thousands of miles of our federal interstate highways system. Too, other threads of our transport system, such as the familiar Greyhound Lines founded in 1904, are intertwined with economic threads. The constrictive threads of profit and service that required Greyhound to close some 850 stops and plan the closure of an additional 150 in small isolated communities are targeted because they follow an unworkable business model.

In the avionics industry, a tapestry is being layered for the world's first standards for sense and avoidance systems, adopted by the U.S. Department of Defense, to lessen aircraft mishap collisions. Unmanned aircraft systems, aircraft platforms, network control, are in developmental stages, extended multi-purpose platforms to float at 25,000 ft. altitude.

Among the kaleidoscopic constellation of major societal tapestries, one merits particular attention, the golden arches of McDonalds' the world's largest fast food company.

San Bernardino, California was the site of the first McDonald's in 1948. Dick and Mac McDonald signed with Ray Roc in 1954 the brother sold the franchise in 1961 to Roc. 1962 the billionth burger was sold. In 1967, the company moved outside the U.S. to Canada. In 1968, the Big Mac was introduced. The 1970s saw an additional 500 restaurants created. The first Ronald McDonald House, the temporary residence for families of hospitalized children opened its doors in 1975.

The vast size and overwhelming success of the Golden Arches of McDonald's consist of many strong threads in worldwide societal tapestry. There are threads of prompt service, easily recognized menus, clean available restrooms, and price levels corresponding with the budgets of much less than affluent customers.

It is surprising that many do not recognize or appreciate the subtle community relationships which are nurtured by the Golden Arches. Retired seniors seize opportunities to enjoy informal coffee klatches with friends, parents take time to observe their children in the secure play areas. Recognition of traveler's needs is reflected in the restaurant's location, easy access, parking area, and access for impaired persons.

Recently, my wife and I, during a 3,500 mile auto trip, principally along interstate highways stopped at McDonald's in a number of states. In Texas, we chatted with refugees from hurricane Katrina. They needed modest motel accommodations and modestly priced food. They appreciated McDonald's services.

Our small and admittedly informal sampling and comparing of results confirmed our conviction that McDonald's understands and skillfully responds to community and traveler needs alike. Yes, this is a stochastic judgment, but we are convinced it is accurate. The Golden Arches of McDonald's serve as a model of successful achievement within the societal fabric.

Denouement

A handful of yesteryears passed while I struggled to create a book containing meaningful kaleidoscopic views of our planet Earth, together with a brief description of select activities undertaken by humans.

Now that my task has been complete, it is stunning to be confronted with new problems, attitudes, events, and inventions, such as the European Organization for Nuclear Research (CERN). They created the world's largest atom smasher to make discoveries into the nature of "dark matter." Or consider U.S. economic difficulties. It is estimated that the present annual cost of interest on our national debt is in the neighborhood of $200 billion.

The four examples that follow illustrate current issues especially worth of concern.

1. *Terra firma* (Latin = firm land) This expression has long been applied to our Earth with a feeling of safety. However, it is now being labeled "terror" *firma* because of recent monstrous earthquakes battering Haiti, Chile, and Turkey. Our Earth's diameter, approximating 7,800 miles, is now experiencing deadly infirmities, especially within the Pacific Northwest coast, and may produce major tsunamis and earthquakes threatening major cities, such as Seattle, Portland, and Vancouver. Also within the U.S., the subterranean presence of the word's largest super volcano, Yellowstone, is located under a glacial lake that has been slowly

rising since 2004 and is described as having the power of 1000 Hiroshima-type nuclear bombs.

2. Seven Pillars of Wisdom: "Wisdom hath built her house, she hath hewed out her seven pillars," as it is written in the Old Testament, Proverbs 9.1. The testament does not specifically identify wisdom's choice of each of the seven pillars. Identifying God and family as two of the pillars may encourage further identification of the pillars.

3. America's Indigenous Indian: "Few have been more marginalized and ignored by the government as long as Native Americans, our First Americans." – President Barack Obama, White House Tribal Native Conference, November 5, 2007. President Obama's efforts have been received positively. "We respect you as a man of your word," said Jefferson Keel of the National Congress of American Indians." Will the day soon come when we shall hear, again, Martin Luther King's thunderous cry of racial freedom, voiced by an indigenous American Indian: "Free at last, free at last: Thank God Almighty! We are free at last!"

Many years ago I was privileged to work with California's public works and highway representatives. On one occasion a meeting was called to determine which of two proposed routes should be chosen to serve transportation needs. Eight of us were asked to participate.

The meeting lasted nearly two hours. A host of pro-con issues collided. Heated voices were raised. Suddenly, the senior manager pounded the table. The room became quiet. In a heavy, booming voice, he said, "Enough! This issue is too important to discuss!"

I have attended services in American churches, and have had the privilege of visiting magnificent cathedrals and churches in Europe and glorious temples in Asia. I have seen crushed religious structures and monuments in Mexico,

Central and South America.

For years, I have fought the feeling of anger that the smashing of civilizations such as the Aztecs, Incans, and Mayans, and the fact that it involved not only Spanish invasive savagery, but was initiated and supported by Papal church degrees.

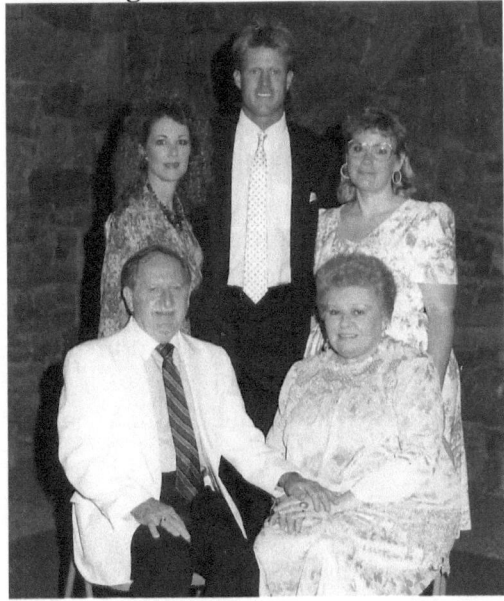

Dexter MacBride and Family

Consider the Papal decree in 1455 that authorized Portugal to invade, search out, capture, and vanquish all savages and pagans along the west coast of Africa and to place them into slavery and take their property.

In 1493, Pope Alexander VI issued a decree that "divided the world from the North to the South Pole," wrote R.J. Miller, a professor at Lewis and Clark Law School, who says it guaranteed "ownership by Spain of all lands to be discovered west of the line, for the expansion of the Christian rule."

It is heart-rending to learn about the great number of lawsuits recently filed against Catholic clergy because of unthinkable criminal acts. Sex abuse scandals are not confined to the U.S. The Catholic Church in Germany and Ireland is receiving similar information of abuse and cover-ups from the 1930s to the 1990s, involving more than 1,500 children.

In the Christian world, it is recognized that the 'Sermon

on the Mount' is the most valuable, powerful, and treasured sermon ever offered mankind.

Among the many treasures, there is one that has long fascinated me; concern that we not pray in public, rather "when thou prayest, enter into thy closet and when thou hast shut they door, pray to thy Father which is in secret; and thy Father which seeth in secret, shall reward thee openly." (Matthew; 6:6)

Jesus discusses the second step, "The Lords' Prayer," and the 3rd contains the beautiful simple, golden sentences: "ask and it shall be given you; seek and ye shall find; knock and it shall be opened unto you."

With the clear, specific simple steps, think what might be used to protect, improve, and strengthen our nation, a country that has astounded the world since 1776 with our pledge to all citizens; "Life, Liberty and the Pursuit of Happiness."

Three crystal-clear adjurations from the Sermon on the Mount include:

- Where to Pray (closet)
- What to Pray (Lords Prayer)
- How to Pray (ask, seek , knock)

It is time to conclude this commentary:

Our Water Planet called Earth is the stage for mankind. Our entry, performance, and exit are but flashes of nanoseconds.

Benedictus Qui Venit In nomine Domini!

www.ingramcontent.com/pod-product-compliance
Lightning Source LLC
Chambersburg PA
CBHW020745180526
45163CB00001B/355